James

Tired, Tested, Torn, and Full of Faith

Study Guide | Five Sessions

Micah Maddox

Harper*Christian*
Resources

James Study Guide
© 2023 by Micah Maddox

Requests for information should be addressed to:
HarperChristian Resources, 3900 Sparks Dr. SE, Grand Rapids, Michigan 49546

ISBN 978-0-310-14108-2 (softcover)
ISBN 978-0-310-14109-9 (ebook)

HarperChristian Resources titles may be purchased in bulk for church, business, fundraising, or ministry use. For information, please e-mail ResourceSpecialist@ChurchSource.com.

First Printing April 2023 / Printed in the United States of America

23 24 25 26 27 LBC 5 4 3 2 1

Contents

Introduction

Life was slipping through my fingers faster than I could catch it. I tried to grab it all up and hold it tightly, but it was dripping through my grasp day by day. I felt it most in the people around me. Yesterday my children fit perfectly in my lap. Suddenly they awkwardly hung off the edge of the sofa bigger than I ever remembered before. My parents wrestled with health problems that I couldn't fix no matter how many times I showed up. The wrinkles in my forehead showed signs of a thirty something creeping up close to forty something. And my body was changing so quickly that my jeans were hard to pull past the middle of my thigh. Life would not stop. Until it did. Dad's cancer moved fast.

Maybe you've heard the saying, "Live everyday like there's no tomorrow." People say it and it sounds good both spoken and written, but when you see it being lived out, and watch the literal life being poured out of a person who lives and breathes deep in their faith even when their own life is fading, it's miraculous. God's plan for us to be the salt and light comes shining through so brightly you can literally taste it. And I did. The salty tears streamed down my face over my top lip and right in my mouth as I watched Dad share Jesus until his breath was gone. The taste is unforgettable. Faith so rich, it can't be forgotten. It leaves behind a taste, a memory, and legacy that lasts. So we are faced with the question, how do we live like that? How do we go from tired, tested, and torn, to full of faith?

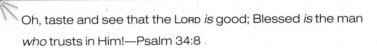

> Oh, taste and see that the Lord *is* good; Blessed *is* the man *who* trusts in Him!—Psalm 34:8

Maybe you know the taste of hard faith all too well. You've faced a battle or ten in your life and you know what it's like to feel like your faith is lacking or maybe even lost. Sometimes when life hits us hard, we are spurred on to live with a fiery passion and rich faith. But eventually we move beyond the fresh passion of living with full faith and we get into the regular rhythm of life again. Life moves on and so do we.

Days and weeks flutter past and Christmas decorations are already on the shelves of the stores, again. The new year sits on the horizon and we desire change this time. Real change. We want to make this year the one that counts. You know the year I'm describing. We've all begun again at some point only to rest in the rhythm of regular all over again. But not this time. It will be the year you finally lose that weight, get serious with God, and do all those things you've always wanted to do because you are feeling mighty full of faith this year.

Losing my dad taught me a lot, but one thing that stands out is how faith is tested when we face circumstances that rock and wreck us. Perhaps it's not a person you have lost, but maybe it's a job, relationship, dream, or a baby that never came. Maybe a faith-filled tear has fallen over the edge of your eye down your face one too many times and you are sitting in the seat of wanting to trust God more, but struggling through unanswered questions, prayers you keep on praying, and life circumstances that can't be fixed. This is why I wrote this book—it's for you.

It's for the ones who know what it's like to suffer more than once. It's for the ones who know what it feels like to have a heart that is broken and wonder if life will ever feel good again. It's for the ones who know God can fix it, but struggle to wonder why He doesn't. It's for you and if I'm honest, it's for me, too. I've sat in the seat of grief, suffering, and wondering how my faith that feels tested and ripped from corner to corner will ever make it. And I've lived through it to tell you, you are going to make it. James teaches us how to live filled with faith even when we don't feel like it. Grab your Bible, a pen, and a friend who wants deeper faith and let's dive into week one.

WEEK
ONE

Full of Faith
When Life Won't
Let Up

Day One: Faith's Purpose

Last week I sat in a doctor's office as the doctor looked down at the test results in her lap and she told me the only option for me was major surgery. In the depths of my heart, I wanted my faith to shine without any fear, but the truth is my faith was the last thing on my heart and mind. I felt worried and anxious. I was even a little angry that God would allow this to happen.

Do you ever feel like you can't take one more thing? I mean, you're on the edge. Your nerves are shot. Your mind is done. Your body is tired, and your emotions are a mess. If you could gather yourself for a moment, you might explode at the reality of all you've been through. Life is hard.

I have no doubt you have experienced things in your life that have taken you face-to-face with your biggest fears and heartaches. I have too, and yet somehow I still know there is a bigger picture and purpose for it all.

When we want our lives to matter and our days to count, and trials come out of nowhere testing our faith, it feels frustrating to think the faith we thought we had isn't enough. In the face of our struggles, we have a choice. We can play it safe and seek comfort in what we think we can figure out, or we can examine our hearts and realize our deep need for more authentic faith. The problem is sometimes we have an unrealistic idea of what real faith looks like.

I try to check off my *good church girl* list of do's and don'ts like reading my Bible, praying through a prayer list, attending Bible Study, and going to church to prove to myself and to God I have big faith. I might even take it to the next level and promise God I won't gossip, cuss, or insert my opinion unless asked as to say I'm really getting serious about my relationship with Jesus and using "God-given" discernment. I feel like if I can do more for God, He will do more for me. Somehow when I feel like I'm following the rules, I think my faith is really getting traction. But I'm learning most of the time when rules are the focus, I still feel like God is distant, and the anxiety in my chest pounds harder. I cannot check off enough boxes to ever feel truly full of faith and close to God. I'm left feeling like I'm waiting on God to fix my problems and calm my anxious heart.

> But let patience have *its* perfect work, that you may be perfect and complete, lacking nothing. —James 1:4

I want to introduce you to one of my favorite people in the Bible. He has a lot to say about rules and the unexpected, out-of-your-control life struggles. His name is James. Scholars believe he was the half-brother of Jesus (the son of Mary and Joseph) and according to Scripture he was an important leader in the early church. He was writing to a group of people who believed Jesus was the Messiah they had been waiting for. The tension found in James' writing is birthed out of a deep history of Jewish customs and practice. While the Jews had once been following the Old Testament law, now Jesus' death, burial, and resurrection had done away with the Jewish law and made a way for *all* to come to Christ. This merging of Jew and Gentiles now *both* able to receive equal grace, mercy, and forgiveness freely from God through Jesus was a new way of faith. Not only were there new believers, but as the church grew and believers multiplied so did their persecution. Those who did not believe Jesus to be the Messiah were causing much chaos and trouble for those who did believe.

Throughout our time together we will learn a few things that James says produces a life full of faith even when life is hard. He doesn't hold back on the facts and gives some direct instructions to hold onto in order for faith to be full and active. He's a straight talker who gets to the point and doesn't sugar coat or soften the facts that make faith work or worthless. If you are ready for your faith to feel full again, this book is for you.

If you've been tested one too many times and the grief grips you when you least expect it, you will find direct instructions to get moving forward on your faith journey. You don't have to live feeling torn up all the time. You can live a life full of faith even when your heart has been tried and tested. Elizabeth Elliot so eloquently put it this way, "The secret is Christ in me, not me in a different set of circumstances."[1]

James gives us a lot of principles to live by and ideas of what holiness means. He makes it clear that good works do not equal nearness to God. **The works we do should be the fruit of our faith rather than the foundation for it.** This is the message James was offering the believers he addressed. And this is our lifeline to walk in deep faith. When our purpose is secure in Christ, our actions prove it.

When we choose to live from the foundation of faith in Christ, everything else flows from that choice of faith. When we choose works, life is about rules and regulations. A life touched by Jesus should reflect deep faith believing what His word says is true that salvation is by grace alone, not works.[2] James will offer some insight into how we can live fully in the grace, mercy, and truth of salvation as our foundation of faith rather than a by legalistic regulations that hold us captive and consume our attention and efforts.

When the heart is tired, tested, and torn from corner to corner, what's deep inside will flow out of it. This is when the real message of James comes to light. Do we live in deep faith that is growing, active, powerful, and able to offer patient understanding and wisdom through it all? Or do we wrestle with the bumps in the road that make us feel uncomfortable, hurt, and knocked down?

As we walk through the book of James, we will reflect on the teachings of Jesus from the Sermon on the Mount and the wisdom of Solomon from days gone by. As we see how these life principles intersect and repeat, we will gain a new understanding of the whole counsel of Scripture and the timeless truth of sincere faith.

> But be doers of the word, and not hearers only, deceiving
> yourselves. For if anyone is a hearer of the word and not a
> doer, he is like a man observing his natural face in a mirror;
> for he observes himself, goes away, and immediately forgets
> what kind of man he was. But he who looks into the perfect law
> of liberty and continues in it, and is not a forgetful hearer but
> a doer of the work, this one will be blessed in what he does.
> —James 1:22–25

At first glance you might think James is saying "work harder to have deeper faith," but the message tucked beautifully within these short five chapters is that faith rests in a heart devoted to God. It's not about more rules, but rather a deeper relationship with our Father and Creator. This is where we will discover how to truly make our days count. It's not so much about what to do or what not to do. It's more about how to live fully in a relationship with the One who created you to use your moments to count for eternity. Even the difficult moments. For it's in those moments that we draw closer to Jesus and realize our soul's need for help.

Charles Spurgeon describes James' teaching like this, "We are very grateful to James that he is so downright, so straightforward, so plain and practical. He never minces matters. He hits the nail on the head every time. Whenever he talks about faith, he seems to be saying all the while, 'Believe;' if he discourses on prayer, you can hear him crying, 'Pray;' and if he speaks concerning holy living, you can hear the thunder at the back of his words commanding us to forsake sin and to follow after righteousness."[3]

You are going to want to grab a copy of your Bible to follow along in our time together. Each week I will give you a portion of James to read to start the week. Don't skip this important step as it will give you the full picture of what will be coming up in our study. For each day of this study,

I will offer questions for deeper understanding, personal application, and a prayer to conclude our time together. At the end of each day there is a memory verse for the week. Take time every day to apply your heart to memorize the verse of the week so when life hits you out of nowhere you have a word of defense in your soul. Write it on a sticky note, put it in your phone, and apply it to memory.

Today will look a little bit different as we briefly lay the foundation for James, but get ready. We will dig in deeper day by day.

If you want to invite a friend to read along with you or a group to study together, the questions each day are a great point of conversation and reflection. There is nothing sweeter than having a friend to walk through this faith journey with, so enlist a friend or ten friends and let's get started.

> So teach *us* to number our days, that we may gain a heart of wisdom. —Psalm 90:12

Imagine numbering your days. Day 1–birth. Day 2 . . . What would each of your days look like? For some the beginning is precious and priceless. A day of joy to two wonderful parents. For others your heartache began in the womb before you even had a chance to take your first breath. We all have a story and every day of our lives has shaped who we are today. Your life matters (no matter how good or how gory) and what you do each day will exhibit how deep your faith really is. If your life is anything like mine, there are many days that have been wasted on worry or wounds that can't be fixed. There are days that could be labeled by depression, anxiety, anger, fear, oppression. While yes, I've had some victories, the days that stand out when I really start counting are the hard ones. The ones where my faith has been tested. The ones where my heart has been challenged. So today, I just want to ask two questions that stem from Psalm 90:12 before we really dig into James.

Apply It

 If you truly lived like every day counted, what would you change right now?

 If you could describe a heart of wisdom, what would it look like?

The common ground we can stand on today is that every day of our lives matters. With each new day, we will face new circumstances that will challenge our faith. It might not be a doctor's report, but the struggles, losses, and battles are often bigger than we can handle. Through it all we need a heart of wisdom to see beyond ourselves and beyond this moment. It's a journey of patient faith that will carry us from one battle to the next increasing our faith time and time again.

Prayer of Faith

Dear Heavenly Father, I want to live a life of faith. I want my life to count and my days to matter. Help my heart to be tender and my mind to be open as I study the book of James. Give me fresh understanding and new wisdom to see your truth and grow my faith. In Jesus' name, amen.

Memory Verse

But let patience have *its* perfect work, that you may be perfect and complete, lacking nothing. —James 1:4

Day Two: Faith's Test

I was in the seventh grade. The bell rang as I awkwardly slid into my seat. The teacher stood before the class and said, "Get out a blank sheet of paper and a pen." The pop quiz had not even started and I knew I would fail. Pop quizzes have never been my strength. I had not taken my books home. I had not read over my notes. I didn't even truly pay attention the day before. I mindlessly copied the notes from the board and went on with my day. I sat faced with a test I wasn't prepared for. As the questions were asked, the frustration mounted. I had no idea of the answers. The final question came and we passed our papers to the person behind us to grade. When I got mine back, it was just as I expected—a big fat red "F" for failure.

I wish that "F" stood for "faith." As an adult, I don't slide awkwardly into my seat for pop quizzes anymore, but I do find myself sitting uncomfortably in the seat of tests and trials I never saw coming. I feel the heat rising up my neck and my heart beats a little faster when unexpected circumstances pile up. I hear my heartbeat in my ears and I wonder if I'll make it through this trial stronger this time or end up breaking under the pressure of the unexpected. There is no letter grade to tell me how awful I've done at preparing for what is ahead. I wish I could say I am always strong in faith and never fail the tests that lie before me, but I do fail.

What if I told you James gives us a better way to deal with the pop quizzes of life and the tests we face that we never saw coming? No more sliding awkwardly into your seat hoping for a better grade. No more stomach turning, shocked face when life hits from out of nowhere. Let's see what James has to say when life offers a pop quiz. Get your Bible and pen ready to take notes. Don't worry, I'll help you with the answers.

Digging Deeper

As we look at key verses in James, there will be important ideas, patterns, or unique lessons to notice. God's Word is so rich, we can't possibly cover everything, so I will give you the highlights and we will dig into specific topics that point us to deeper faith. Don't get hung up if you don't know the answers right away. I will do my best not to give you questions that leave you wondering what I want you to answer. These questions can simply help you look at God's Word and see what James is saying to his original audience. Then we will apply the Bible truth to our own lives in real time and cling to the truths we discover.

James' opening words hold key context for us in understanding who he is talking to and why he is sharing the points he is attempting to make.

Open your Bible to the book of James and read James 1:1–12.

 Who does James "greet" as he begins his writing?

It's important to notice the twelve tribes were Christian Jews who had been "scattered" throughout the Roman Empire due to current persecution. There are two things to note:

- The people he spoke to were Jewish Christ followers. There was a Christian presence throughout Jewish communities, but they were not all in one local community, they were spread throughout Gentile nations.
- The struggles they were facing were current. Jewish customs were woven deep into the fabric of the Jewish culture. The Christian Jews now faced the conflict of following Jesus over the rituals and regulations once followed according to Jewish customs. James was one of the earliest written works to the Christians (before Paul's letters).

James wasn't speaking to something they had already made it through, but what they were walking through currently. They were in the middle of the pop quiz and James was giving them the encouragement and answers they needed right then for the test they faced. It's not as if he was looking back over all the trials they *had* faced, he was encouraging them in real time as they walked through it. This is what God does for us in our trials.

God gives us what we need when we need it. He doesn't watch us wrestle until we can't take another step. If we seek Him through His Word, He gives us exactly what we need right then. His presence and His Word offer comfort and help to get us through life's most perplexing problems. As the Christian Jews faced persecution from the Roman government, conflict of belief with family, friends, and neighbors, and the challenge to know what they believe and why, James gave real-time hope, instruction, and encouragement. His focus was on how to stand up and do right regardless of nay-sayers or tradition. It was a countercultural message to live according to what Jesus taught over Jewish law and customs. It was not a live better because you are better message, it was a live better because Jesus in you is all you need and with Him you will be able to live blessed rather than oppressed by the current situations at hand.

Apply It

 Has God ever provided what you needed just when you needed it? Maybe it was a song, a sermon, a verse, an item, money, or a kind word from a friend or stranger. Write down a time or two when God provided exactly what you needed at just the right time.

How does it encourage you to know God provides in your time of need in this season of life you are in right now?

 In what circumstance or "pop quiz" of life do you need God most right now?

 Fill your name in the blank. God gives _____ what she needs when she needs it.

Prayer of Faith

Dear Lord, I need you. Life can feel unpredictable, and I am weary with all the tests that keep coming. Encourage my heart to remember You give me exactly what I need when I need it. Show me today that You see me and are in this test of life with me. In Jesus' name, amen.

Memory Verse

But let patience have *its* perfect work, that you may be perfect and complete, lacking nothing. —James 1:4

Day Three: Faith's Waiting

The kitchen was piled high with moving boxes. Each one was filled full with the things of our lives and taped shut ready to go to the next place we would call home. We stood arms around each other smack in the middle of the boxes and lifted up a prayer for the day. While all seven of our lives were packed away for the moment, we were in the middle of a storm. It wasn't one thing that burdened our hearts. It was a season of life when struggles hit from every side.

I know you know what I mean. It's when the enemy hits you in the gut, the nose, and knocks your feet right out from under you when you least expect it. It might be the unexpected job loss, divorce papers that hit you from out of nowhere, perhaps a diagnosis you didn't see coming, or an addicted child you never dreamed in your worst nightmare would hit your family. Or maybe you've been through something I could never even fathom and put into words. That's the way some storms hit. It's the unexpected crazy stuff that no one would even believe.

Our trials piled up in their own way. We were moving a family of seven which is never easy and seldom uneventful. Selling a home sounds fun until it's not. Everything was on schedule to close the deal when we got the call that there was water found in the crawl space of the home we were selling. Thousands of unexpected dollars were literally going down the drain to make the deal go through. We were facing a huge court date for our foster baby and the outcome and possibilities weighed heavily on our hearts. A child we loved as our own was literally in the hands of our state's justice system. We held her tightly not knowing if she would stay with us forever or leave at any moment. In the midst of it all, my husband woke with a spider bite on his leg or so we thought. When the spider bite grew and another one popped up, he went to the doctor, which led to a biopsy, and waiting for results. This waiting and carrying burdens beyond our control is an exercise I don't love.

Maybe you've been there. Perhaps you've stood in the kitchen with boxes to the sky just waiting to move, or maybe in the waiting room of a hospital or hospice center, perhaps the courtroom, or an unimaginable room where suffering seemed like it would never stop. We've all been there in one way or another. **The key to difficult seasons in life doesn't rest in what we go through, but how we grow through.**

Seasons of standing in the kitchen arms wrapped around each other, saying goodbye to places and spaces of refuge, waiting for phone calls with results we have no control over, anticipating judgments and edicts on our lives teach us about ourselves and about God.

- About us—We can't make it on our own or in our own strength. We need each other.
- About God—We need God's strength because we are weak. We need the Lord's presence because we cannot live life without Him.

God cares about the little things like moving boxes, tape, and markers. God cares about the big things like biopsies, court outcomes, and how we will ever get through all this stuff that seems too hard to handle.

It's not that God has left us to figure it all out on our own. It's that God has given us His Word and Spirit to guide us through when we don't know what else to do.

One of the beautiful things about God's Word is the way it all works together for one common goal and message. The book of James is just one proof of that beauty. As we dig a little deeper each day, some days we will look to the words of Solomon and David in the Old Testament, and others we will observe Jesus in the New Testament and see how the truths James offers were not only for the Jewish Christians that were enduring trials and temptation, but also for the generations to come. The lessons Jesus taught echo the wisdom of Solomon and the heart of David from years before. **Today we hold in our hands a Bible that offers wisdom not only for patriarchs of the past, but also for the present—for us.** We have everything we need to endure any hardship that comes our way.

Digging Deeper

Open your Bible and read James 1:2.

I find it ironic to read about counting or considering joy in the midst of difficulty. Joy is the last thing on my mind when I face hard times. I don't want to make a gratitude list or look on the bright side when everything around me seems dark. I tend to melt into the pit of sorrow and pout my way through each day. Maybe you know what it's like to wear your emotions on your sleeve, or perhaps you have a friend or family member whose mood you can identify from a mile away. We all have our days when we just can't fake it anymore.

Circle the responses you typically run to when circumstances rock your world.

Anger

Fear

Resentment

Prayer

Calling a friend or family member

Busyness for avoidance

Worry

Escape in food, drink, or other pleasure

Shut down

Counseling or therapy

Medication

Entertainment

Other _____

For me, I like to be alone. I pull back. Shut down. Stop trusting and confiding in others. I get angry, and while I am very aware that God is able to help me through the trial, my typical response to unexpected struggles is usually worry, anxiety, and fear. I think of every *what if* and *what now.* Joy is not my first reaction and I imagine the people who were enduring persecution had some similar feelings going on.

Sometimes I even ask God, *why?*

When I instruct my children to do something, this is the little question that lingers between the instruction I give and the action I expect them to take. "Why?" Although they know I might respond in some situations with "because I said so," there are other teaching moments when a reason is practical and helpful.

For example, "do not run out in the street to chase a ball, toy, or dog without looking both ways." While I could answer with a simple, "because I said so," a better teaching moment might include a simple explanation of the result of what could potentially happen if they do not heed the instruction. The result of disobedience is potential disaster and even possibly death. While this sounds a little extreme, it is reality. This same idea is found here as James teaches the people why they should consider joy when they are tested.

Knowing that the testing of your faith produces patience.
—James 1:3

According to James 1:3, what is the "why" or the result of considering joy over something else in the face of trials?

There are true heartaches and deep traumas that knock the wind out of us, and joy can feel very distant. There is a reason James is offering such an audacious promise of satisfaction. He has experienced joy only found in Jesus. But this did not come easy for James. James was the brother of Jesus. He lived with a perfect person in his house. Can you imagine? How could he compete with that? It took James years to learn and receive the truth about Jesus. His joy in Christ didn't come immediately. He was not born with it. He had to choose faith in Jesus just like you and me. Yet, he had a history with Jesus like we could never even imagine. On one hand you might think it would be easier for James to have faith in Jesus because he saw him up close and even lived with him, but the storyline we find in the Bible gives us a different outcome. Let's take a look at a few verses that show us some facts about James' history and faith.

 Read Matthew 13:55–56. Write down the names of Mary's children that you find.

 Read John 7:1–5. What do these verses tell us about Jesus' brothers?

Take note that this disbelief from his brothers is taking place after Jesus has performed multiple miracles and just months before his crucifixion. It's difficult to understand how they couldn't be amazed and caught up with faith. Perhaps they were so close to Him, they had made up their minds what they believed about Him before He truly displayed His power. This is both convicting and compelling for us to evaluate our view of who God is and what He is capable of. When we put God in a box and decide what He can or cannot or will or will not do for us, we are trying to forge our own faith. Or maybe a better way to say it would be to forfeit our faith. God is bigger than we can manipulate or imagine.

Read 1 Corinthians 15:7, Acts 1:14, Acts 2:1–4, Acts 15:13.

There is a lot happening within these verses, so let me give you a short summary. After Jesus' resurrection He appeared a few different times. One of those is noted in 1 Corinthians 15:7 when He appeared to His brother, James. In Acts after Jesus has ascended, we find James on the scene with the other believers being filled with the Holy Spirit, and finally in Acts 15 we hear James addressing the Jerusalem council. What is really interesting here is what James had to say. He makes a bold claim that the message of Jesus Christ does not require the law, but abstinence from such things as offerings to idols, meat of some animals, and sexual immorality *are* considered in how we receive the message of Christ. James warns against these behaviors, but never claims they are required *for* faith in Jesus. Culture-driven behaviors are most often not evident in a true believer's life. If we assessed even non-believers on morality, we would find some abstaining from these things. James makes the point to focus on faith in Christ first over the fear of the law.

This is where we find the real heart of James' message in his book of the Bible. **The principles James gives aren't required *for* faith, they are more the result of a life lived *from* faith. Faith changes our behaviors.** Let this message of mercy penetrate your thoughts as we look at all the things he instructs as guidelines for us to live by.

James' introduction of joy even when we are tired, tested, and torn gives us a new way to approach the subject of faith. He doesn't leave us to wonder how we accomplish the task of a joy-filled, faithful life. He gives us the answer straight away. But it's not easy.

The answer to *how* we respond with joy resides in James 1:4, "But let patience have *its* perfect work, that you may be perfect and complete, lacking nothing." Completeness in Jesus Christ comes only as a result of faith that waits and rests in God alone.

Patience is the pathway to joy. This is a hard truth because patience might be one of the most difficult character qualities to practice and perform. It's not a natural response and it definitely does not come easy for most of us. Just take a look around during a traffic jam or observe a long line at the airport terminal when all flights have been canceled. Waiting is so hard. With Jesus, we can practice patience by trusting Him no matter what. Even when we have to wait longer than we expected for answered prayers. Even when we have to wait longer for healing. Even when we have to wait longer for a breakthrough. Even when we have to wait longer for the relationship we've begged God for. When we wait in faith, we begin on the right path toward joyful living.

Apply It

Today, we take our first visit to the scene of the Sermon on the Mount. Jesus is teaching and sharing some difficult concepts. This one comes toward the end of a section called the Beatitudes. As He describes what it looks like to live truly blessed, He includes a nod to James' lesson about having joy during persecution.

 Read Matthew 5:11–12. Write down one or two things these verses tell us we should do in response to persecution.

While it might be easy to pull a statement from these verses to answer the question, it is much more difficult to actually live out. Sounds a lot like exercising true faith. Pursuing patience and joy through suffering requires a faith that is willing to wait. It means when we sit in the waiting room or the seat of suffering, we uncross our arms, let our jaws relax, and open our hands and hearts to consider the possibility of having joy over the circumstances.

When have you been challenged to wait for something? What was your response? Be honest whether you waited well or waited wallowing in anger, self-pity, or any other attitude.

Today, choose joy in the waiting. Rejoice where God has you and know every day you are alive you have a purpose. It might not look like you imagined. You might even find yourself in a kitchen filled with boxes and an uncertain future, in a family that looks dysfunctional, or even a waiting room that makes you feel like this trial will never end, but even here God is at work. His best work is often done in the depths of a heart that desperately seeks Him while it's waiting.

Prayer of Faith

Dear Heavenly Father, I want to wait well. I know and believe you work all things together for good, but sometimes it's difficult for me to understand why You allow some things. As I learn to sit in the waiting room, give me faith to keep trusting even when it's hard. I choose to consider joy over my pain, my past, and my problems today. I choose to seek and see You working even when life feels hard and complicated, even in the waiting. In Jesus' name, amen.

Memory Verse

But let patience have *its* perfect work, that you may be perfect and complete, lacking nothing. —James 1:4

Day Four: Faith's Desire

I bowed my head and could feel the stress in my body from my head to my toes. I didn't know what to do. I wanted to make the right decision and do what God wanted me to do, but I didn't know what the right thing was. When life hits from every direction and chaos seems to be the norm, it's difficult to see a clear path forward. Maybe you've been there wrestling in your soul trying to figure out the next right step. You weigh the pros and cons, you read the articles, and search the Web, but still, you battle for a clear answer. Obstacles loom at every turn and the struggles seem too many to overcome. What now? What next?

James offers good news amidst the bad news of any difficult circumstance. It's simple and direct, but it's good news. "If any of you lacks wisdom, let him ask of God, who gives to all liberally and without reproach, and it will be given to him" (James 1:5).

You can be wise. You can make sound decisions and live in God's will even when life seems to tear you to pieces. There is no magical wisdom only reserved for a chosen few. God in His mercy offers wisdom to all His children who ask Him.[4]

Digging Deeper

James tells the believers they simply need to ask God for wisdom. This biblical principle of seeking and asking God for wisdom is not new. We can trace it all the way back to the Old Testament in 1 Kings.

In 1 Kings chapter 1, David was nearing the end of his life and it was time for a new king to be crowned in Israel. David crowns his son, Solomon, as the new king (1 Kings 1:34, 39). Shortly after he became king, Solomon had a dream. In his dream God came to him and told him he could ask God for anything. He could have asked for wealth, or health, or victory over all his enemies, but instead Solomon asked God for something much more valuable—he asked for a discerning and understanding heart to judge the people well.[5]

Read 1 Kings 3:5–13. In verse 7 what does Solomon call himself?

Solomon took a step of humility. He told God, I don't know it all. Say these words out loud wherever you are right now, "I don't know it all." It's a hard truth to admit sometimes. If you are anything like me, when stress mounts, and hard times come, even though I know in my heart that I don't know it all, I go into control mode. I try to control what I can and I do all I can to get things in order. After all, where there's a will there's a way, right? But God is teaching me, **where there is His will, there is a need for His wisdom.**

Admitting we don't know everything is a good place to begin our faith journey. Just as a child has to let go of their own will and surrender to the authority of parents, so do we to God. When we become like a little child ready to receive wisdom from God and God alone, we are taking a huge first step toward deeper faith.

 Solomon teaches about wisdom in Proverbs 2:1–6. Read through each verse and underline the action words. I've done the first few to get started. Each action will give us something the "son" is supposed to do when it comes to wisdom.

My son, if you <u>receive</u> my words,
And <u>treasure</u> my commands within you,
² So that you <u>incline</u> your ear to wisdom,
And <u>apply</u> your heart to understanding;
³ Yes, if you cry out for discernment,
And lift up your voice for understanding,
⁴ If you seek her as silver,
And search for her as for hidden treasures;

⁵ Then you will understand the fear of the LORD,

And find the knowledge of God.

⁶ For the LORD gives wisdom;

From His mouth come knowledge and understanding.

Proverbs 2:1–6

Notice how each action word is a step we can take when we are seeking **God's wisdom**. Solomon knew the key to actively **receiving God's** wisdom was actively **seeking God**. When we seek God, we find Him and all He offers, wisdom included. Jeremiah says it this way, "And you will seek Me and find *Me,* when you search for Me with all your heart."[6]

Apply It

Imagine you go to the doctor and hear you have a new diagnosis. What is your first step when you get in your car to drive home? If you are anything like me, you go straight to Google. Always searching for answers, timelines, symptoms, and cures. You read the articles, listen to interviews, and long for answers.

There is so much information out there, it can be difficult to practice seeking God first. We have so much access to information. It is often difficult to discern between information and wisdom. But the difference between the two is the source of the information. Only God gives true wisdom. The famed and adored theologian Charles Spurgeon said, "We are all so ready to go to books, to go to men, to go to ceremonies, to anything except to God. . . . Consequently, the text does not say, 'Let him ask books,' nor 'ask priests,' but, 'let him ask of God.'"[7]

There are so many things that take our attention away from God's wisdom. The overabundance of information takes us down rabbit holes and the rings, dings, and pings of our phones cause us to live addicted to a little computer in our pocket rather than the King of Kings. What if we practiced doing better? What if we truly sought God first and fought to live devoted rather than distracted?

Take a look at this list of distractions. While these are not all bad things, they can tend to take a lot of our time and attention.

Family problems	Busyness	Children
Relationships	A cram-packed	Spouse
Activities	schedule	Education
Information online	Mental clutter	Weather
Social Media	Shopping	Mental health
Hobbies	A messy house	Entertainment

Now look back through the list and circle your top three distractions. Maybe you could choose all of them, but I want you to pick only three. Don't get caught up here too long. Quickly choose which ones you nodded at as you read through the list. Some of these things are good things, they just overwhelm us and cause us to lean toward living with a divided focus. It's so easy to focus on all the tasks we have to complete, all the places we need to go, and to all the people we are responsible.

 How do we live devoted to seeking God's wisdom in the real world?

 According to James 1:6, how should we ask God for wisdom?

Faith is a predetermined decision before you hit the fork in the road. It's a devoted life that says, I will seek God first and walk with God throughout my day. It's a surrendered heart that knows God will take care of it before you even find out about it. **Wisdom says, I don't know it all, but God sure does.** This is wisdom. It seeks God and finds Him to be present and always there. Wisdom tells the heart the truth about who God is and who you are. It reminds you to take a deep breath, pray, and remember all things work together for a greater good because God is good.

 Name two areas of your life that you need God's wisdom right now:

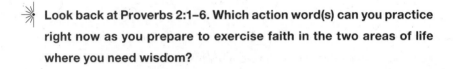 **Look back at Proverbs 2:1–6. Which action word(s) can you practice right now as you prepare to exercise faith in the two areas of life where you need wisdom?**

Maybe you, like me, need to have a Solomon moment with God every single day by saying, "I _am_ a little child; I do not know _how_ to go out or come in."[8] In your own words, write a sentence or two that expresses this same thought in your current situation:

_____

_____

_____

Prayer of Faith

Dear Heavenly Father, I know I do not always turn to You first when I need wisdom. Please forgive me for seeking worldly wisdom and trying to figure things out on my own. Help me seek You with a sincere heart and a devotion that casts out all doubt. Give my heart a steady desire to seek Your wisdom first and when I forget, remind me. In Jesus' name, amen.

Memory Verse

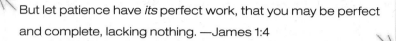

But let patience have *its* perfect work, that you may be perfect and complete, lacking nothing. —James 1:4

Day Five: Faith's Action

Today's study is a little different. We are going to take a look at a portion of Scripture that might be familiar to you. Anytime we walk through difficult stuff it is easy to throw a Band-Aid Bible verse on our battle wound and try to press on, but actually pressing on is much more difficult. Rather than pressing *on*, I want to encourage you to press *in*. Once a week in our study we will take time to personally reflect and impress on our hearts what we are learning. Today we will take the time to read through one short familiar chapter of Psalms and see what it offers us as we think about our faith being put to the test.

Take a minute or two and read through Psalm 23 out loud. Read every verse slowly as if it's the first time you've ever read it even if it is familiar to you. I've provided it here for you:

The Lord *is* my shepherd;
I shall not want.
He makes me to lie down in green pastures;
He leads me beside the still waters.
He restores my soul;
He leads me in the paths of righteousness
For His name's sake.

Yea, though I walk through the valley of the shadow of death,

I will fear no evil;

For You *are* with me;

Your rod and Your staff, they comfort me.

You prepare a table before me in the presence of my enemies;

You anoint my head with oil;

My cup runs over.

Surely goodness and mercy shall follow me

All the days of my life;

And I will dwell in the house of the Lord

Forever.

Digging Deeper

For our Digging Deeper section, I want you to take out a pen and do a quick little exercise to help your mind receive and remember the truth we find in today's reading.

Write out Psalm 23.

_____

_____

_____

_____

_____

_____

_____

_____

_____

_____

_____

_____

_____

_____

_____

_____

_____

Some versions of the Bible conclude Psalm 23:1 with "I shall not want," while others say, "I lack nothing." Both give us the idea of complete contentment. This is the same idea we find in James 1:4 when James says, "But let patience have *its* perfect work, that you may be perfect and complete, lacking nothing."

☀ **Fill YOUR NAME in the blanks below:**

The Lord is _____ Shepherd, _____ shall not want.

The Lord is _____ Shepherd, _____ lacks nothing.

Surrendering our hearts and lives to the leading of the Lord as our Shepherd positions us to live content, satisfied lives completely full of faith. This is the change that happened in James when he chose to follow Jesus. No longer did he worry about winning, sinning, or wining and dining. He now had a reason for living that was beyond himself and beyond the circumstances he faced.

When we choose to live content with Jesus, we choose to live in deep faith even when life hits us hard. It's faith that is willing to wait, be taught, and exercise waiting all over again and again.

Faith isn't something we can muster up when life gets tough and trials hit. **Faith is a decision made in the heart before the trials pile up. It's choosing Jesus before we feel desperate.** It's seeking God before cancer, divorce, or devastating loss.

Maybe you are smack in the middle and feel like it's too late. It's not. While seeking God first is always the best, God in His mercy is available to you right now. It's not time to give up and say it's too late. It's time to declare with bold faith, that you will consider it all joy and seek God's wisdom over everything you are walking through. Here are a couple of my favorite verses to encourage you to take the first step.

Apply It

Read Psalm 27:13–14 and Romans 8:28. How do these verses encourage you to wait in faith?

What is one trial you are walking through right now that is requiring you to exercise patience, wisdom, and deep faith?

Prayer of Faith

Dear Lord, as I walk through circumstances I never anticipated, remind me You are near. Strengthen my faith as I practice patience and seek Your wisdom. Help me remember Your truth and Your presence is always available. When I feel like no one understands, remind me You see me and know exactly what I am walking through. In Jesus' name, amen.

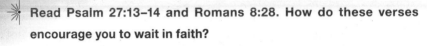

Memory Verse

But let patience have *its* perfect work, that you may be perfect and complete, lacking nothing. —James 1:4

Full of Faith to Hear from God and Follow Through

Day One: Faith's Character

Before we jump into our study today, take out your Bible or open your Bible app and read James chapter 1. I know we already covered some of these verses in our time together last week, but reading the full chapter will help lay the groundwork for this week and build on what we already studied.

Heart thumping and hands shaking I entered the doctor's office. They handed me a pink robe and a clipboard of paperwork. I pulled back the curtain of the tiny dressing room and changed into the robe and filled in every blank on the paper. My heart was terrified. What if the lump I found was more than just a lump? What if I only had a limited time to live? What if I faced treatment that would make me sick and affect my daily activities? All of the fears of what might happen flooded my mind and I was melting into an anxious puddle ready to cry at any moment.

I moved from the tiny dressing room to the waiting room stocked with snacks, coffee, water, and intentional beauty. The artwork seemed like it was supposed to be peaceful and the ambiance of the lighting appeared like it was planned to offer calmness. But I was anything but calm. It wasn't time for small talk when sitting beside a stranger with nothing on but a shirt-robe. It wasn't the most relaxed I had ever felt. I sat side by side with others all waiting for the same test with the same fear and same hope. We each sat with eyes straight ahead, unable to speak.

I worried and I was afraid of the results. This trial marked my life in a noteworthy way. Like a wave of the ocean, I was carried to a place of anxiety like never before. The rush of each step in the doctor's office took me deeper and at one point I felt like I could not breathe.

My results came and the wave of relief was more than I could bear. Negative. My lump was just a lump. Nothing scary. Nothing to worry about. Simply something to note and watch.

Maybe you've been there in a place where the weight of life seems to sit on your chest so heavy and you feel like you might have to gasp for air. Or maybe you've drifted out to the sea in a state of worry and anxiety that threatens to take you deeper than you feel you can swim. Perhaps your results were much scarier than mine and you've walked a road no one ever chooses or wants to walk.

I think you probably can relate in some way to the heart thumping fear that consumes your life when you least expect it. This is where faith and fear seem to collide. You might know in your mind that you should have faith that God is going to work everything out, but you also know in your mind the real possibilities of what *could* happen. You either lean hard into faith, or get lost in anxiety.

This brings us to James 1:8, *He is a double-minded man, unstable in all his ways.* As we observe James' description of a double-minded man, to make it more personal we will say a double-minded lady. Bible scholar David Guzik gives a great explanation of the wave of the sea mentioned here and gives four qualities of the wave that help illuminate the danger of living a double-minded life. He says, "A wave of the sea is a fitting description of one who is hindered by unbelief and unnecessary doubts. A wave of the sea is without rest, unstable, driven by the winds, and is capable of great destruction."[1]

Take a look at each of these qualities and think about your life. Have you ever felt any of these when you faced uncertain circumstances?

1. Restless
2. Unstable
3. Out of control
4. Filled with fear

There is a better way to live. By deciding to live with faith as our guide rather than fear, we are choosing a steady life free from the roller coaster of crashing waves and temptations that welcome disorientation and chaos.

Digging Deeper

We could easily say, "Have more faith" or "Be strong." But I think there is more to faith than a Christian cliche or a little word of encouragement. To confidently walk into an unexpected life event without being driven to great depths of fear and anxiety or taken under by a wave disillusionment, you need a firm foundation of faith.

A firm foundation of faith might look something like this:

- Know God's Word and take Him at it.
- Choose God's promise over the pain.
- Live loved when life makes you feel unloved.
- Lift your head to look to Jesus when life knocks you down.
- Press on when life presses in.

This is faith in action. It's not a wishy-washy indecisive faith. It's a faith that knows God sees, God hears, God is there, and God is faithful. We have a decision to believe faith will carry us through. **Double-minded faith is undecided faith.** Living double-minded is living with a self-sufficient attitude. It's an *I can do it myself* kind of life. This kind of thinking will not help you through the storms but will only keep you in them longer. Faith in God means I choose God to lead and be the Lord of my life even now when I cannot figure everything out. Without this decision of choosing faith in God, fear will always take over.

Take a look at these verses in Matthew from the Sermon on the Mount.

"Ask, and it will be given to you; seek, and you will find; knock, and it will be opened to you. For everyone who asks receives, and he who seeks finds, and to him who knocks it will be opened."
—Matthew 7:7–8

In this excerpt from Jesus' teaching, there are three metaphors Jesus used to explain how God provides for His children.

 For each one, write the result Jesus gives from Matthew 7:7–8.

- If **you** ask, it will be . . .
- If **you** seek, you will . . .
- If **you** knock, it will be …

If you look back at Matthew 7:7–8 a little closer, there is a word found in each of the examples that gives us a look into God's care for us.

 Do you see the common word? (Hint: It's in bold above.)

God cares individually for **you.** Not only does He care, He wants you to receive answers from Him. He knows your name and the number of hairs on your head or lack of them. He sees every tear you cry and every tear you hold back. He cares about what you will do today and tomorrow and the next day. Before we are ready to receive from Him, we have to decide we want Him more than anything else.

This means you have to want God more than trying to figure out how everything is going to work out. It means you want God more than an answer or a reason why. It's faith in practice and pursuit. It's knowing when you knock on the heart of heaven, God hears and loves you. It's knowing when you seek God, you'll find Him in a fresh way through His Word, His presence, and His peace. Wanting God is about beginning to understand that His presence is enough to soothe the empty hole in your desires.

Sometimes living double-minded comes so naturally, we don't even realize we do it. We practice it when life goes wrong.

Life hits, we worry.

Life happens, we whine.

Life hurts, we get angry.

We ask all the hard questions.

As we ride each wave up and down, God is steadily reaching out His hand offering peace, rest, and calmness. Our hearts don't have to live anxiously terrified about what might happen. Life will give us reasons to worry, but faith says, I trust God even in the little pink robe. Even with the lump. Even with the results. Even with the outcome. Even with the next wave or the next lump.

I don't know what you are facing today, but I do know there is a choice you can make. How will you ride the wave when you feel anxiety creeping in? You can ride the wave of faith. Or you can ride the wave of fear. One leads to peace and the other to a deep ocean of water that will terrify you until you can't sleep or function.

Faith knows fear is coming and chooses God's peace over the possibilities.

Apply It

What is one life event that has gripped your heart with anxiety or worry in the past?

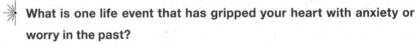 What do you need most from God in this season of life? Maybe peace or rest. Or perhaps direction? Write it down and be specific.

✳ **What is one way you can practice living in faith over fear?**

✳ **From Matthew 7:7–8, which one do you need to practice most in this season? Asking, seeking, or knocking?**

✳ **What will the result be if you practice faith rather than fear in the situation you struggle with most in this season?**

Prayer of Faith

Dear Lord, life hits hard sometimes and I don't know how to handle it with strong faith. I want to be strong and not be tossed like the waves, but I don't always get it right. Please help me in this situation to rest in You. I am deciding today to choose faith over fear. To ask, seek, and knock on the door of heaven rather than my own strength. I need you today. In Jesus' name, amen.

Memory Verse

But he who looks into the perfect law of liberty and continues *in it*, and is not a forgetful hearer but a doer of the work, this one will be blessed in what he does. —James 1:25

35

Day Two: Faith's Reward

I have a love-hate relationship with water. I want to drink more water, but when I have the choice, I often turn to the highly caffeinated option like a cold Dr. Pepper or iced coffee. I get a little bolt of energy and then bam! Sugar crash. It happens every time and yet the choices I make continue to consume me and make me choose the sugary drinks over and over. Even though I know I will only receive temporary satisfaction from that cold Dr. Pepper or Dunkin Donuts iced coffee, I still open the fridge and look for that cold drink or drive to the closest coffee shop to satisfy my need. Maybe you are more of a Diet Coke girl or a hot tea lady. Either way, most of us can relate with the struggle to choose the things we know are better for us over the things that make us feel good for a quick minute.

> Blessed *is* the man who endures temptation; for when he has been approved, he will receive the crown of life which the Lord has promised to those who love Him. —James 1:12

Just like I struggle with the first few days or weeks of a new pattern of making good choices for my health, I also struggle with making new choices for my heart. Do you know the feeling?

As we dig into our study today and discuss temptation, there is a great reward offered to those who handle temptation appropriately. For some of us, we have to learn the hard way. We are the ones who are addicted to our favorite cold drinks, or who struggle with making healthy options for our minds and bodies over and over. But this promise of a reward makes me sit back and evaluate how I can do better.

One biblical truth God keeps showing me is this. **Obedience to God breeds blessings. Disobedience to God breeds destruction.** Does this mean my life is over if I disobey God? Absolutely not. Your life is not over or ruined or incapable of being blessed. This is where deep faith intersects with mercy and forgiveness. It's taking yesterday's decision to live by faith and resisting temptation today because of your deep desire to obey God.

The gospel message is for all sinners. Jesus' blood covers all sin. Those who choose Jesus are ultimately choosing God's eternal blessing. Within that choice to follow Jesus lies a blessed life of obedience. This is why James gives us so many life principles. He knew and experienced life before belief and blessing. Therefore, he also experienced a sinful life. This is why we hear him urging the believers to stop living like unbelievers and to step into the blessed life they say they identify with. He is warning them about living a double life because he knows the outcome is far from living blessed.

Digging Deeper

 Psalm 1 has much to say about the blessed person and the ungodly person. When we see God offering a blessing it is usually connected with that person doing what is right. In the space provided use Psalm 1 as your guide to describe the blessed person and the ungodly person. Go through each verse and jot down a few facts the Bible gives us about each one.

Blessed Person - Psalm 1:1–3	Ungodly Person - Psalm 1:4–6

When we remember God's truth about living a blessed life, we live more equipped to practice the obedience of faith. Choosing faith when life knocks the wind out of us is not an easy choice. Everything in our human bodies tells us to be afraid. Our hearts beat faster. Our temperature rises. Our insides want to eat everything or nothing at all. Life is hard on the body physically. If we are not equipped spiritually, obedience in the face of temptation will feel too difficult to conquer.

If we can learn how to deal with temptation before we face it, we will be equipped to make the right choice. It's kind of like preparing your food choices ahead of time. If you know you are going to a party or out to eat and you are trying to lose a little weight, you might predetermine you won't have dessert or you won't drink the sugary drink. But if you don't decide ahead of time, that tempting double chocolate cake or cheesecake drizzled with strawberries will look too good to turn down. Don't get me wrong, I am not the healthiest eater, but I do see a clear comparison between how I care for my physical body and my spiritual health.

Scripture like James 1:12–15 convicts my heart to stand up and want to resist temptation when it comes. But the problem is I am not always ready to defend myself when the enemy comes to tempt me. Just as I don't prepare my water bottle for the day ahead or predetermine I won't go through the drive-through for a quick meal, I often don't take time to predetermine how I will defend my heart from the strong pull of Satan on my soul. How can we be ready when we are face-to-face with temptation?

The best example I know to follow is Jesus. In Matthew 4 we find Jesus being tempted by the devil. Not only does Jesus show us how to respond, but He also gives us the answers we need in moments of our own temptation. Let's see what we can uncover from His answers to the devil's ploy to get Him off track.

 Read Matthew 4:2–11.

While this portion of Scripture is not within the Sermon on the Mount, it is recorded directly before it. Jesus walked through being tempted in multiple ways directly before one of His most noteworthy messages. Isn't that the way life works sometimes? If we can make it through the temptation, there is much for us to do for God on the other side.

 Look back at these specific verses in Matthew 4 and see if you can find the common theme.

Matthew 4:4
Matthew 4:7
Matthew 4:10

Each time Jesus responds to the devil, He responds using the Word of God. This is not a coincidence or just a cute idea, it's invaluable to our understanding of how to resist the devil's schemes in our lives.

 Look up and read Isaiah 40:6–8. What are our lives compared to in these verses?

 Read James 1:11. What similar idea do you see to Isaiah 40:6–8?

 What stands forever according to Isaiah 40:6–8?

The Word of God gives us every answer and weapon we need to stand up in the face of temptation. And the reward for standing and not giving in to temptation is blessing and a crown of life. Some of us are motivated by positive reinforcement, but it's in the weak moments that we will need more than the hope of a star on a star chart or a pat on the back. In order to stand strong and not give in we must be armed with the Word of God. In order to be armed with God's Word, we must know God's Word. How can we use God's Word as our defense if we do not know what it says? I imagine this is one of the reasons you are doing this study, to get to know God's Word in a deeper way.

When we live disciplined to be in God's Word, we reap the benefits. The reward is a pure life, filled with living water that cleanses and purifies the soul. While I might still give in to my cold Dr. Pepper or afternoon coffee, my heart and soul isn't worth the heartache of a quick moment of weakness that leads me to sin. Lord, help us stand up with Your Word as our sword and source of strength and truth in the face of temptation.

Prayer of Faith

Dear Heavenly Father, I need You. As I walk through my day, I want to guard my heart and mind with Your Word. I want to pre-decide that Your way is better than my way. Bring to mind Your Word as I fight each battle today. Help me remember my strongest defense is not my words, but Your words. In Jesus' name, amen.

Memory Verse

But he who looks into the perfect law of liberty and continues *in it*, and is not a forgetful hearer but a doer of the work, this one will be blessed in what he does. —James 1:25

Day Three: Faith's Foundation

You were created by God for God. Let those words sink deep into your soul today.

Say these words out loud: "I am created by God for God."

Say it again, "I am created by God for God."

I know you probably know this, and I don't need to tell you, and it might feel silly to say it out loud but sometimes it's good to remember where we come from and why we are here. I don't mean your hometown or family roots. I'm talking about who formed you from the beginning of time. Before your mother even knew she was expecting you, God already had you in mind.

In Psalm 139:14 we read the psalmist's words. He reminds us we are fearfully and wonderfully made. In Jeremiah 1:5 the prophet is reminded that God knew him before He formed him in the belly of his mother. Just as the people in the pages of Scripture were formed by God and known in the womb before they were born, so were you. You are an amazing creation of the Almighty God.

You might find it strange to find the harsh truth of temptation that we discussed yesterday followed by such a comforting truth that we are God's amazing creation. Sometimes it is difficult to allow the beautiful grace of God to mix with the judgment of God. But this is where we must learn to receive the truth that God is both just and merciful.

While yes, He offers forgiveness for all sins, He also tells us over and over there are consequences when we give in to temptation. This is the warning James is offering in this small excerpt of chapter 1. While James gives the reminder that the people are God's amazing creation, he also gives a strong instruction to listen and exercise specific disciplines lest they live in deception toward their own lives. It's an interesting perspective to consider.

Immediately following the gracious talk of how God is the Creator and men were brought forth by the Word of Truth, there is a bold instruction of how a follower of Christ can endure difficult circumstances.

The way James stacks up the instructions gives us a wonderful cumulative understanding of how true faith is revealed in a Christian's life.

As we look into today's study we are going to walk slowly through each verse and see what James has to offer.

Digging Deeper

James 1:21 holds the key to the foundation of our faith. It's where our faith is born and where it lives. Before we dig in to verse 21, let's lay some groundwork and explore what James is communicating to the people. Open your Bible to James 1:17.

 Read James 1:17–18. According to James 1:17–18, by whose will were the people created?

This is a foundational building block to our understanding of God's plan. He is the creator of all mankind. He is the one who creates life. This is a basic truth we build on as we define real faith. We cannot move forward in our faith until we agree that God created all things, including you and me.

 Look at verse 18 again and write down what James says they were created *from*?

It is by God's will and God's Word that creation is possible. In Genesis we find God spoke the world into existence (Genesis 1). This is important and reminds us of the value of God's Word both in times past, and in times present. If we do not value God's Word and esteem it with reverence and belief, we will feel stuck and unable to exercise deep faith.

 Look at verse 18 one more time and write down what they were created *for*?

James points back to the purpose for life. Perhaps this group of believers were becoming distracted, and dissension was beginning to take root. James was giving them the needed reminder to keep the main thing (Jesus) front and center. This sounds oddly familiar to our modern-day Christian experience.

While we strive to serve God and build the church of God, there are so many things that come up along the journey that take our hearts and minds off of who created us. We forget where we came from and why we are truly here. **Serving is not about staying *busy for* God, but it's about staying *focused on* God.**

When we look at this message from James and reflect on our own lives, we can give ourselves as an offering to God. As we surrender our whole selves to God, we can serve with the right motives and sincere faith. This is learning faith that lasts beyond the heartache and heart-breaks. It stands strong through the storms and keeps focused on the foundation of faith rather than the fears, failures, and formalities of man.

"Therefore lay aside all filthiness and overflow of wickedness, and receive with meekness the implanted word, which is able to save your souls." —James 1:21

James goes on to give another warning. He instructs the people to do two things in verse 21. List them here:

 As a result of setting aside the sin they are holding onto and accepting God's Word, what is the result of these actions? (Hint: It's the final phrase in James 1:21.)

Apply It

This "Christian" lingo is used often in our churches when we say, "I got saved" or "Are you saved?" This is one of the verses where we get this shortened phrase that represents the choice to follow Jesus Christ as Savior. There are other ways you might have heard it said, such as:

Are you a Christian?
Have you decided to follow Jesus?
Is Jesus your Savior?
Do you believe the Gospel?
Have you asked Jesus into your heart or into your life?
Are you a follower of Christ?
Are you a believer?

James reminds the people where they came from, so they know how to move forward as children created by God. This was a big deal for the Jews who now followed Jesus as the Messiah they had been waiting for. James gave them direct instructions to let go of the customs they once held onto for faith and was teaching that there is no greater truth to remember than the truth of their salvation through faith in Jesus. What Jesus did for them changed everything. It literally saved them not only from eternal hell, but from a life of striving. With active faith ready to listen and receive God's truth, James says they can count it all joy. But they must remember where they came from and where they are now. Basically, he says don't forget how you have been saved, redeemed, and reborn into God's family because of Jesus Christ.

 Record your salvation experience here:

Note: If you have never made the choice to follow Jesus, today can be the day. Admit you are a sinner. Ask Jesus to come into your life as your Savior and Lord. Choose to follow Him today. He will meet you where you're at and you will see.

 What hope does living in Christ give you?

Take a moment to thank God for your salvation and remember the way you felt when you realized how much God loves you. Write down a word of thanksgiving here:

We cannot live through trials, testing, and struggles without knowing our foundation of salvation.

This message from James gives us a clear reminder that there must be a laying down of sin and turning point toward the Word. This is the redemptive power of God's great love for us. The result of receiving the Word is living saved. It's not just saved from hell but it's living saved to a life of faith. Because we are forgiven, adopted, and redeemed by Jesus, we have what it takes to live differently—a new identity, a new source of hope, a newfound freedom in Christ. To live found, free, and for God.

Prayer of Faith

Dear Lord, I don't want to just talk about faith, learn about faith, and look at what a life full of faith might look like. I want to live it out. Thank You for Jesus, my Savior and my foundation. Help me remember You, my Creator, as I live my life each day. Help me focus on You and remember why I do what I do. When I start to mouth off and talk too much, help me remember to listen more than I speak and to do more than I talk about. In Jesus' name, amen.

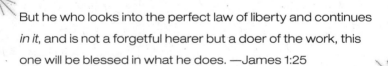

Memory Verse

But he who looks into the perfect law of liberty and continues *in it*, and is not a forgetful hearer but a doer of the work, this one will be blessed in what he does. —James 1:25

Day Four: Faith's Wisdom

I glanced over at my husband's phone and saw a message containing one of those funny gifs. I think there is a debate about how you pronounce this new word in the English language. Either you say it with a "j" sound or the traditional "g" sound is up to you, but I tend to think it's a "jiff" pronounced like the brand of the peanut butter. If you look it up online, you'll find either pronunciation is acceptable.[2] The message that contained the gif was a conversation with a woman at my church. I knew this woman. I was even friends with her. But immediately I wondered why in the world he would be sending her a funny gif.

I also tend to be a little bit of the jealous type, therefore I can get irrational when I encounter a situation that makes me think crazy things. I didn't say a word, but rather let my anger get stirred up until a couple days later when I couldn't hold it in any longer. Yes, an entire couple of days. I know we aren't supposed to go to bed with unresolved conflict in our hearts, but it takes me a little time to process things. So, I let it linger and the longer it lingered the angrier I became. Then I finally said it, *"Why are you texting that woman funny gifs?!"*

He looked at me like I was crazy. "What in the world are you talking about? I didn't send her that gif. She sent it to me."

I grabbed the phone and looked back at the text message. Sure enough I had it all wrong. He wasn't crossing the line like I thought. He was innocent. On the other hand, my anger shifted from him to her. After realizing she sent the gif and looking back at the text, I realized it was most likely innocent and completely ridiculous that I got so crazy mad. I did keep a close eye on her from then on, but nothing else ever came of it. No more funny gifs and no more crazy outbursts as a result. I know you might think I'm a little overboard at this point, but I like to call it passionate.

Maybe you're not the jealous type. Maybe you don't care one bit about silly gifs. But one thing I know we can relate to is jumping to conclusions and letting ourselves get all worked up over things that are not worth spending our emotional, mental, and spiritual energy on. Have you ever found yourself in a tizzy and just about to light someone up only to realize it wasn't really what you thought after all? Misunderstandings happen most often because we assume things that aren't true. James must have known this would be a struggle for us. He left us a reminder, right here in the midst of remembering who we are and where we came from, to be slow to get angry and be slow to speak our pieces.

Digging Deeper

Read James 1:19–20.

Different translations of the Bible use different words for the sake of common language used by the reader. No matter what translation you are using, we are going to revisit a few original Greek words to get the idea of what James was teaching.

What are the three instructions given in these verses?

- Swift to _____. The Greek word for "swift" is "tachys" which figuratively means quick or prompt.[3]
- Slow to _____. The Greek word for "speak" is "laleo" which means to utter a voice or emit a sound.[4]
- Slow to _____. The Greek word for "wrath" is "orge" which implies the temper or anger.[5]

What does James imply the result will be if they do not heed this warning? (James 1:20)

In simple terms, James is saying, you cannot live faithfully if you cannot control your mouth and your anger. This takes us back to that decision to live a life of faith and resist temptation. Often, we think faithfulness is being heard, speaking up, and speaking out. While there is definitely a time and a place to speak the truth in love, there is great wisdom in adopting this three-part principle to life that James teaches.

1. **"Quick to listen" means ears are open and mouth is shut.**

   It's a hard lesson to learn. You've probably heard the saying, "Open mouth, insert foot." Imagine walking around with a big ole foot in your mouth. Your message can't be received from others because they cannot even understand what you are saying. It is too muddled through the mumbling you are producing with that big thing in the way.

2. **"Slow to speak" means you think first.**

   I've learned this the hard way, too. As a teenager I began to learn I had a voice and I started using it. But when I loudly mouthed off a slang word I didn't really know the meaning of in front of the entire high school, the reaction I received was humiliating. My friends could not believe I said that word. And I couldn't either even though I had no idea what it meant. I learned a big lesson that day. Don't say things when you don't know what you are talking about! Many times it is better to keep your mouth shut.

3. **"Slow to anger" means you live with patience and wisdom.**

   Once again, this is a hard learned lesson. There are certain things I am super passionate about. You have your things, too. It's those things that get your heart racing as soon as the topic is brought up. And you feel like you need to speak your mind. For me it's things like foster care and bargain shopping. I feel strongly about these things and sometimes want to give my opinion even if my opinion is not requested. If the topic is brought up, I will share my two cents. And sometimes that is exactly about how much it is worth—two whole cents.

I am learning it is often best to let others go first with their words, listen, and oftentimes just let it be without interjecting my opinion. We all have developed and are developing our own ideas of what is right and what is worth talking about. James says, slow down! Listen up! And just sit down. That is where you will exercise righteousness. It's not in proving you are right or knowledgeable or even passionate. **Let passion compel you to "do" rather than "speak."** When we live out our passions rather than just talk about them, that is when we will be heard.

Apply It

 Read Matthew 5:43–44. How does the lesson James is teaching here about slowing down and listening rather than blowing our tops and running our mouths mimic the teachings of Jesus?

What does Jesus teach our response should be? Not only slow, but what else should we do?

It's easy to read the words, "Love your enemies." But it's so much harder to actually live them out. It takes great faith to slow down and let God's Word and truth permeate your heart in the circumstances that get your blood boiling. This is when we must remember who we are in Christ. Because of Him, we can rest in Him and we don't always have to speak our minds or be heard. The outcome of slow to listen, slow to speak, and slow to anger brings peace beyond our imagination. I dare you to try it. I'll be trying my best today too, and only by God's grace will any of us succeed.

Prayer of Faith

Dear Lord, help me be swift to hear, slow to speak, and slow to wrath. When I get all worked up about something that isn't worth getting worked up about, help me to remember to listen rather than speak. Guard my heart and my mouth so I can think clearly and speak only when You say so. In Jesus' name, amen.

Memory Verse

But he who looks into the perfect law of liberty and continues *in it*, and is not a forgetful hearer but a doer of the work, this one will be blessed in what he does. —James 1:25

Day Five: Faith's Discipline

It was one of those days. The kind when everything hits all at once. The list of things to be done was long. Time was short. The day seemed to rush by and nothing went my way. I wanted to slow down and live in the faith I knew by surrendering my angst to God as I tried to muscle my way through the one hundred things on my to-do list, but my flesh took over and before I knew what was happening I was hollering at my kids and making a royal fool of myself in word *and* deed. It is one thing to make a fool of yourself in front of your family but an entirely different thing when it's public. And that is what happened this particular day.

I know you've probably never done this. I'm sure I'm the only one who has ever totally lost it on the people I love the most (insert graceful sarcasm). But there I sat loudly and passionately giving my children a piece of my mind. Before I could finish one of my sentences, I glanced across the room to notice the window was open. Not only was the window open, but our new neighbors were taking a walk and happened to be passing by right as I escalated my volume to an all-out passion filled yell. You can imagine what I sounded like. I used to be a cheerleader so I can get loud! Sheesh.

The worst part was we had recently invited them to church. They knew we were Christians. They knew my husband was one of the pastors at the church. I hoped they heard the good part about how I was trying to teach my kids a lesson and overlooked the ridiculous tirade I was on. I can confidently say I was living in complete rebellion to the lesson James teaches in James 1:22. I knew I should not provoke my kids to anger or lose my temper, but I had lost it. My nerves were shot and like a lightning storm I let my thunder crash violently over my house.

This is a prime example of hearing and not doing. I have heard countless messages and read books and blogs about how to be a godly mom and great parent, but this was not my finest moment. This was a moment when I forgot whose I was and what I was created for.

Ever been there? Maybe you aren't a mom with kids who push you over the edge, but you have co-workers, family, or even acquaintances that make you want to scream every once in a while. It's those passive-aggressive social media posts that get under your skin, or the undermining comment that hits you where it hurts. Maybe it's just the way a person breathes or chews that irritates the ever-living snot right out of you. No matter what it is, we must be willing to admit it and own it. We get worked up over stuff and sometimes we just lose it.

> But be doers of the word, and not hearers only, deceiving yourselves. —James 1:22

To both hear the Word and do what it says requires more than a little faith. It requires discipline. It's a daily choice to wake up and remember who and whose you are. It's a practice of patience that resists the temptations to blow up and lose your mind even when you feel justified in doing so. While we all can probably tell of a time or two or twenty when we've maybe forgotten who and Whose we are, this lesson of hearing and doing has the potential to change our patterns of how we hear, receive, and live out the truth of real faith. If we look back at what we've already established, we will remember James has already said to stop doubting what you know is true and pre-decide you will live in faith. Stand up in the face of temptation and do right because you are in Christ. And finally because you are God's, be slow to wrath and slow to speak. When we do, we will be living out all that James is teaching. It's like a snowball effect of knowing what to do, understanding why we do it, and then following through.

Digging Deeper

Read Matthew 7:24–27.

Jesus tells the story of two men building homes. One is considered a wise man. He builds his house on a firm foundation of rock. When the weather gets tough, the wind blows hard and the rain causes flood waters to rise, the house stays standing. It doesn't shift, change, or crumble. Then there is another man who builds a house. Jesus calls him a fool. He builds his house on sand. But when the weather gets bad, the wind blows hard, the rain causes flood waters to rise, the house is destroyed. The wise man had a firm foundation. Jesus said he was like the one who heard the message and did what was taught. The foolish one heard the same message but did not follow through. When life got tough, he lost it.

Oh, how foolish we are sometimes. You might be able to understand my story of losing my temper with my kids because you've been there in a similar situation. But how much better would it be for me to remember the rock that I stand on is not a place to parade in my foolish pride and spout off in my flesh how I really feel. What if instead of losing my cool, I could remember how good God is. What if I could be slow to anger? Is it even possible?

I know sometimes the lessons we find in God's Word can feel almost impossible. Things like keeping your cool can feel hard when life is pressing (especially if you are passionate). But the result of living steadily and strongly in a series of storms proves your faith. Sometimes we think of faith as an exercise of belief only practiced within the walls of a church or in the moments of great sorrow, sadness, or tragedy. But faith in the daily moments of life is the real measure of hearing and doing.

Faith is not only tested when the bills aren't paid, or the dishwasher breaks. Faith is not only needed when a new diagnosis causes fear. Faith is needed when you open your eyes each day and you pull back the covers and put each foot on the ground. What lies beneath you will determine how you live. Are you stepping out onto the rock of your salvation or are you stepping out into your own strength on the sand of your own ability?

Apply It

Read Psalm 18:2 and write down a few ways the psalmist describes the Lord.

Read Psalm 18:30–36. What hope and encouragement do these verses offer as we live to not just hear but do what we know God is calling us to do?

Write out Psalm 18:46 in the space provided and underline the words "my Rock."

As you go through the next week, what is one promise from this week's study that you can cling to that will help you both hear the Word and do it?

Prayer of Faith

Dear Lord, I don't want to step into another day without You as my Rock. Help me when I feel strong in my own strength to remember I am nothing without You. Help me when I feel weak to know You alone are my Rock. I want to be a hearer and doer. When I mess up and lose it, bring me back to the Rock. In Jesus' name, amen.

Memory Verse

But he who looks into the perfect law of liberty and continues *in it*, and is not a forgetful hearer but a doer of the work, this one will be blessed in what he does. —James 1:25

Full of Faith When Life Seems Unfair

Day One: Faith's Warning

Before digging into this week's study, take out your Bible or open your Bible app and read James chapter 2.

We had just adopted our son. He held a cute sign and we all joyfully gathered as our family welcomed him officially to the Maddox home. It was a great day! One we had waited over two and a half years for. We followed the adoption ceremony with a fun dinner at Cracker Barrel and then headed home to get ready to head out of town for a little family trip to celebrate. We got on the road early the next morning. It wasn't long before I realized our newly adopted son was having a hard day.

The details of our son's history are private, but the fallout was in our faces and some days we struggled to know how to help him. This was one of those hard days. His tantrum escalated and there was no reasoning with him. I tried all the things you might try with a young child to calm and soothe him. But he was clearly dealing with more feelings than I could manage in a cram-packed car on a road trip where everything was out of sorts.

We pulled into the gas station to try to help calm him. His screaming had gotten to a full volume as panic was setting in. I opened the van door and tried to calm him face-to-face using every trick and tip I had ever read specific to adoption out of trauma. When I realized my efforts were not working, I thought maybe a change of scenery would do the trick. I pulled him from his car seat. My body now in a head-to-toe full body sweat and my heart racing in frustration because those books had not given me the tools to help in this situation. I was at a total loss. This was supposed to be a happy trip. We were going to spend time celebrating and bonding as a family.

My husband pumped the gas. The other kids took a deep breath as my son (who was still screaming) and I went inside the gas station bathroom to try to calm down. I squatted down in the restroom stall and wrapped my arms around my new son. I told him it was going to be ok and practiced slowing my own heart rate and breathing. As I held him, his little body began to slowly relax, too. We stayed like that until he completely stopped his sobbing and then we embraced one last time, stood up hand in hand, and walked out of the stall.

Tears filled my eyes as I held the heavy weight of raising our new son not knowing how we could ever be everything he needed. But right outside the stall stood a young woman. As I opened the door, before I knew what was happening she wrapped her arms around me. Then she looked me in the eyes and said, "You are doing a great job. You are a good mom. Keep it up."

In that moment I learned what it looks like to love a stranger. She loved me and showed me love even though she had never met me and knew nothing about me or my new son. She showed the depth of her faith by sacrificing herself for my good. She didn't have to speak to me. She could have judged me. She didn't know why my boy was screaming. She could have assumed I was hurting him or had done something to make him angry. But she chose to love and soothe the ache in my heart rather than judge and think the worst.

Sometimes I am guilty of thinking the worst. I don't automatically assume the best of others and I don't typically freely give love away to strangers with screaming children in the bathroom. But the love I was given that day touched my heart in a deep way. It makes me think twice in moments of judgment.

As we unravel James 2, the definition of true faith James discusses can be confusing and hard to discern. Is faith proved by works? Or is claimed faith enough? We must wrestle with the words of James 2:20 that implies works must be present for true faith to be fruitful. We will do our best to clearly glean what the lesson is without getting into the weeds and muddying up a valuable portion of Scripture that helps us evaluate our faith.

It's not that works create faith or that works lead to faith. What James is discussing is the condition of the heart is what really matters.

He's breaking down that we can't effort our way to more faith, but rather *because* of our faith we are compelled to act in such a way as it honors the Lord whom we love so much. Works, or actions in the name of God are not the root of our faith, they are the fruit of it. The root of faith is the belief that Jesus is all we need. Upon this belief in Jesus, our faith is able to stay firmly grounded through the ups and downs of life. Out of this faith our motivations change and therefore our behaviors change also.

This might sound like a lot to digest. Over the next few days we will work through James 2 and discover why the condition of our hearts bears more weight than the execution of good deeds. Hold on tight and buckle up as we get ready to take the first step toward even greater faith.

Digging Deeper

James was writing in a time when the people were socially divided by nationality, ethnicity, race, culture, and customs. It sounds familiar to what we see today. Everywhere we look we can find evidence of division–from the part of town you live in, where you worship, the past you come from, the color of your skin, and whom you vote for. We will always find reasons to divide. Differences do not always mean there needs to be division. Often differences can be opportunities for growth, but often this is the enemy's way to get in the way of clear sight for unbelievers getting to Christ, but also hinder believers from getting along with other believers. In James 2, we find a strong statement right at the beginning to those who believed in Jesus about how to hold or handle their faith.

> My brethren, do not hold the faith of our Lord Jesus Christ, the Lord of glory, with partiality. —James 2:1

In James 2:1, we find a warning about partiality. While the NKJV uses the word "partiality," other translations use the word "favoritism." In your own words describe what partiality or favoritism means.

Being partial can mean choosing a favorite or choosing someone or something with higher respect by choice or favor. James is teaching faith and favoritism cannot fit in the same hands. Hands of pure faith esteem each person the way Jesus does. If you try to hold your favorite people and your faith in your hands together, it is like trying to ride the fence of holiness and unholiness. God does not approve.

Revelation 3:15–16 gives us insight into what God has to say about those who want to water down or compromise His instruction when it says, "I know your works, that you are neither cold nor hot. I could wish you were cold or hot. So then, because you are lukewarm, and neither cold nor hot, I will vomit you out of My mouth." God's Word clearly says He does not approve of mediocre faith, but we must choose which side we are on—hot or cold.

With this in mind, we have a huge responsibility to know where our faith resides. Are we partial to those who have more money, more beauty, more fame, or who look just like us? Or do we treat everyone the same? Stereotypes, racism, and first impressions affect the way we treat others and we do it without even thinking.

When we show partiality by dividing over class, color, or social status, we are practicing the idolatry of preference. It's as if we think we can control who comes to Christ. While we would never say that or want to think we have any part of treating people this way, the idea of dividing over preferences and outward appearances is not new even among believers. These unspoken ways of dividing classes, races, and ways of life date all the way back to James' day.

This is why James uses several words and pictures to demonstrate what favoritism looks like in the Church. God's Word is clear when it says, "all may come."[1] Salvation is not reserved for any single or classified group—all means all. When we begin to exclude, divide, judge, or label people, we demonstrate a posture of works over a posture of heartfelt faith. We think our work is worthy because of who we are working with, the methods by which we are working, the notoriety or success we are receiving. All of these things cause partiality to rise to the surface and a heart that is partial is not a heart surrendered to faith. This is hard truth to talk about because none of us want to think we are that person. Pride tells us we are impartial and it's someone else who chooses by preference or deference. All the more proof we are guilty of partiality even in our distaste of it.

 What two types of people are described or mentioned in James 2:2?

 What are some of the measuring sticks we use in our current day and age to evaluate if someone is rich or poor?

It is so easy to look at the outward appearance and make judgements and decisions because of how people appear. Often, we don't even catch that we are doing it. However, God uses a different assessment tool. In 1 Samuel 16 we find the story of David and his humble beginnings. While he wasn't his father Jesse's first or even seventh pick to bring before Samuel as an option for the anointing as king, God saw David's heart and that is where the virtue was found. This story gives us a peek into God's standard of how to measure one's character, and in turn, one's value.

Read 1 Samuel 16:6–7. What does God tell Samuel not to look at when he sees Eliab?

 According to 1 Samuel 16:7, what does God see when He looks at people?

It can be easy to justify our actions and attitudes about the outward appearance by using the good ole, "God knows my heart" or "I'm just being honest." But that bold declaration is a weighty truth that ought not be used for justification, but instead, for purification. Rather than use it as a way to prove yourself, use it to prune yourself. Ask yourself if your heart is clothed in righteousness, in purity, in goodness, and faith. These are the things that are valuable in God's eyes and will lead the faithful heart to good works without partiality.

The danger we face is we sometimes judge others without even thinking. It takes discipline and God's work in our hearts to see people with eyes of love and compassion rather than judge their behavior and fashion.

We live in a fashion-obsessed culture. It takes one scroll through Instagram to see the obsession with fashion, appearance, and the perception of perfection. People have given themselves the title "influencer" as a way to influence people to buy specific brand names, clothing items, home decor, food kits, and eyelash extensions. We are more biased and bombarded than ever before, and I fear our faith is being adversely affected. The abundance of what we take in eventually spills out.

The judgment James addresses is in a specific place. Look at James 2:1–2 again and write down where James is warning his audience to beware of giving unequal respect or being partial. (Note: Your Bible translation might say "assembly" or "meeting.")

The gathering taking place here is not a Friday night party or a gathering in the streets of friends. In the Greek language the word *assembly* was translated from the word *synagogue.*[2] The Jewish culture was a very segmented group of people, and it was difficult to move from one class to another. This gives us a deeper look into James' audience. They were primarily Jewish believers in Jesus Christ, and he was addressing how they treated each other within the church. He wasn't just speaking a "love everybody" message. He was pointing specifically to when people gather for worship, be sure you are not raising up those who are wealthy and look like they've got it together. But rather treat all with dignity, both the rich and the poor.

 In James 2:2, how does James describe the rich man?

There are certain ways we evaluate who has money and who lives with less. Our measuring stick might be boats, houses, and cars. Perhaps diamonds, handbags, or name brands. "In Roman society the wealthy wore rings on their left hand in great profusion. A sign of wealth, rings were worn with great ostentation. There were even shops in Rome where rings could be rented for special occasions."[3]

While we can't truly measure someone's wealth by what they wear or how big their home is, or even the size of the rings they wear, we do draw assumptions by how they present themselves. But in our looking at the outside and drawing conclusions we do a disservice to both the rich and the poor.

 Read James 2:8. Who does James instruct the people to love?

It's not that we can't love the rich man or the one who has it all. It's more that our love should not be swayed because of what someone has or doesn't have. The love we have for others should flow from deep faith and love for God. That love is pure and peaceable. It sees beyond the external and reaches the wealthy, the weary, the worn out, and the ones who can't seem to win.

Apply It

In Galatians 6:10 we find a reminder from Paul that sums up today's point perfectly. It says, "Therefore, as we have opportunity, let us do good to all, especially to those who are of the household of faith."

 Why do you think Paul wrote the last part of the verse? Don't get hung up on being afraid to write the wrong answer. Just share how God is speaking to you through the verse.

How we treat others in the church proves the condition of the heart. If we serve with a heart of faith, partiality will not be displayed or detected. We will love others (all others) like James 2:8 instructs and our faith will flourish. Think of someone in your life who might not have it all physically but needs a little encouragement from a sister in Christ. Reach out and let her know you see her and you love her.

Prayer of Faith

Dear Lord, I want to look at others with eyes to see their hearts, not what they have on and not what they can do for me. Help me look with eyes of compassion and purity. Cleanse my heart when I judge and give me fresh eyes of grace to see without being partial. Help me not to fall into the trap of trying to hold both faith and partiality in the same hands so my heart can be ready to express my full faith in all I do. In Jesus' name, amen.

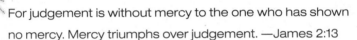

Memory Verse

For judgement is without mercy to the one who has shown no mercy. Mercy triumphs over judgement. —James 2:13

Day Two: Faith's Freedom

We are going to start today with a quick quiz. Get your pen ready and do this first question as quickly as possible. Ready? Set. Go!

 Label each sin in order from worst to not that bad. Start with 10 as the worst and work your way down to 1 being not that bad. Don't take more than one minute. Go!

Sin	Rating
Adultery	
Lying	
Stealing	
Gossip	
Judging others	
Cheating	

Sin	Rating
Showing favoritism	
Hurting someone	
Unforgiveness	
Betrayal	

Maybe you look at a list of sins and think, whew! I'm pretty good. I mean I don't do most of those. And I can't really number them because they are all equally bad. Or perhaps you feel like being dishonest isn't quite as bad as lying (even though they are the same). Or maybe you look at a list like that and think, wow! I'm such a sinner. I've done way worse than any of those.

The truth we will uncover today is found in the amazing mercy of God. While we often hear songs written about the grace of God or the forgiveness of God, there is another attribute of God that James speaks of directly following the firm instruction not to judge others by the outward perception. It's a beautiful word called—mercy.

So speak and so do as those who will be judged by the law of liberty. For judgment is without mercy to the one who has shown no mercy. Mercy triumphs over judgment.
—James 2:12–13

Look back at the list we started with and think about the ones you have done or have been done to you. If we look at the list through the eyes of mercy, we will see it a little differently. With the law of liberty found in James 2:12, the sins in our list are blotted out. It does not mean there are no consequences, no results, or no impacts from the sins on this earth. But it does mean God, rich in mercy, judges you by His perfect law of liberty. It does not mean you have a free pass to sin and do things on the sin list; it means your past does not define who you are. Nor does it mean if you sin God will disown you. This law of liberty not only offers mercy for your sin, but everyone's sins that are covered by the blood of Jesus. When we look at the list through the eyes of mercy, the list looks more like this.

~~Adultery~~

~~Lying~~

~~Stealing~~

~~Gossip~~

~~Judging others~~

~~Cheating~~

~~Showing favoritism~~

~~Hurting someone~~

~~Unforgiveness~~

~~Betrayal~~

MERCY marks each sin without judgment. It is God's deep love for every person over their actions and Jesus' blood that redeems sin. Grace does not excuse sin, it gives each person the opportunity to receive the mercy of the gospel over the judgment they deserve.

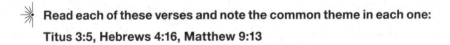 **Read each of these verses and note the common theme in each one: Titus 3:5, Hebrews 4:16, Matthew 9:13**

When I was little, my brother and I would play a game called "mercy." It wasn't a board game or an athletic race. It was simply the act of facing each other, interlocking hands, and yelling, GO! As soon as we said "go" we began forcefully twisting our hands upside down and squeezing and fighting each other with our hands gripped tightly together. The game ended when someone yelled, "MERCY!"

With God we don't play games face-to-face and hand-to-hand, but we do often fight against His will. We push and manipulate and force our way against Him. The interesting part is God always wins, but in His mercy, He allows us to win, too. As His children, we are the ones who have to cry out for mercy, but because of the law of liberty that we read about in James 2, and unlike the childhood game, we win.

Digging Deeper

Let's unpack two things today:

- The gospel according to James 2
- The blessing of mercy according to James 2 ·

The Gospel

Sometimes we complicate what God simplifies. We can over theologize and research until our heads and hearts are spinning. James 2 can be quick to take us into one of those tizzies if we start trying to think too hard.

The goal today is not to confuse, because God is not the author of confusion.[4] But rather, to clarify and simplify the facts of what James is teaching about the gospel.

We've established this far in James 2 that God does not approve of favoritism in any way. He couples this lesson with the law of liberty. When you put the words *law* and *liberty* together it almost seems like they clash. Law gives the idea that there are rules while liberty implies freedom. This is the gospel. We cannot pretend like there are no parameters for those who are in Christ. There are. Let's look at what it means to live in Christ.

> Therefore, if anyone *is* in Christ, *he is* a new creation; old things have passed away; behold, all things have become new.
> —2 Corinthians 5:17

 What old things might Paul be referring to in his writing?

 If all things are new, that means the old ways of thinking, living, and acting are changed. This is what the gospel does. It changes the sinner from sinful to a new creation. Think of your own life and the changes God has brought about. How is your life different because of Christ? Expound on the changes God has brought about in your life because of salvation.

These changes are possible because of God's mercy. He did not have to send Jesus. He did not have to offer a chance for change. In His mercy, He offered a way. Read John 14:6. In your own words, explain why God's mercy is necessary for your life change.

> That is, that God was in Christ reconciling the world to Himself,
> not imputing their trespasses to them, and has committed to
> us the word of reconciliation. —2 Corinthians 5:19

If we are in Christ, our sins are covered by Christ, and we are rec-
onciled to God through Christ. The law of liberty gives us freedom
in Christ because of the gospel. If you are still struggling to put it all
together it might help to remember what the word gospel means.

The gospel means "good news."

It is the good news of Jesus' death, burial, and resurrection that
offers every human the opportunity to live in mercy over judgment and
therefore to offer mercy over judgment to those around them. This is the
reason we share the good news!

In James 2:12–13, James gives those who are in Christ two boundaries to "speak and do" within the law of liberty with mercy as the lens
through which you look at others. If we look through the lens of judgment
with eyes partially to cut down and condemn, we are not living in the
mercy we are offered through the law of liberty or the good news. The
one who has received mercy will be able to show mercy. Or you could
say *the one who has received the good news will be able to share the good news.*

The Blessing of Mercy

When we let mercy rule in our own hearts, we will let mercy rule
in our relationships. The condition of the heart will have its way in our
interactions with others. When we do not let mercy rule, harsh judgment
arises and mercy is canceled proving the condition of the heart is not in
tune with God's mercy. This is when we start judging and criticizing
others because of outward appearances and perceptions.

Perhaps this is why James says, *So speak and so do as those who will be
judged by the law of liberty.*[5] He knew humans might be otherwise tempted

to speak and act in a way that is opposite of mercy. It comes natural to judge others. To pre-decide what we think about others by the outward appearance we see. To jump to conclusions about their past or present circumstances and goals. To think we know what is going on by how they present themselves. The blessing of mercy gives believers another way to live. **Mercy chooses love over looks.**

While we can't control the appearance of others, we can control how we see them. We can choose to see a human in need of God's great mercy and love—the gospel. The problem is not in another's appearance, it's in where our hearts abide. If my heart abides in judgmental thoughts and attitudes, mercy cannot reside there. If my heart abides with the love of Jesus, and I realize the mercy I have been given, I am inspired and motivated to give the same measure of mercy to someone else. Not because I am super spiritual, but because God's mercy works on a heart to break it for the things that break His.

Jesus is always our best example showing us what it looks like to see through eyes of mercy. He saw the people, all of them, and had great compassion. He didn't separate them by what part of town they came from or if they had showered that week. He didn't avoid them because of how they presented themselves.

 Read Matthew 9:36. How did Jesus respond when He saw the multitudes? What was He "moved" with?

He wasn't disgusted or judgmental walking the other way or turning to avoid them. He saw the need of the heart beyond the outward appearance.

Read Matthew 5:7 and Matthew 7:2. What is the result of choosing mercy over judgment?

Until we choose to understand we have received great mercy through our salvation, we will never choose to understand how to see others through the eyes of great mercy.

Apply It

James covers so many different aspects of a joy-filled life, and I wonder if this teaching point from him to the church was one of the most important. While it's good to endure hardship, remember your salvation, and guard your tongue, withholding mercy from others and exercising harsh judgment divides, cuts down, and causes people to question if your faith and God are truly loving and good like you say.

This is why we see James say, *Mercy triumphs over judgment.*[6] Mercy wins. It brings unity. It does not excuse away sin. It simply chooses the truth of the gospel that Jesus died for all. Until we change our measuring stick from man's way to God's, we will never understand mercy. Mercy does not discriminate. It walks in no matter how broken, how bruised, how battered, or poor and says, "Jesus died for you, too."

If we could only look at people with those eyes, our hearts would live much more satisfied. With eyes of judgment we are never satisfied, always seeking who sinned the most, wondering about the latest gossip, seeking out the biggest sinner.

Mercy says, I have sinned and received a great salvation. Rather than, you have sinned and you are clearly a sinner. It's more about receiving our own identity as a gospel-saved sinner than determining who in the room is in need of mercy. When we offer mercy to all, our hearts have taken a huge step toward truly living full of faith.

Read Hebrews 2:1–4. How do these verses encourage you to live as you remember the good news over judgment?

 Take a moment to thank God for His mercy in your life. Write a short prayer that expresses why you are thankful for God's mercy.

Prayer of Faith

Dear Lord, thank You for the mercy You have given me. I know I deserve judgment for my sin. I know I have failed over and over. As I walk through my day, give me fresh eyes to see others the way You see them, with mercy triumphing over judgment. When I am tempted to judge, remind me of the mercy You have given me. In Jesus' name, amen.

Memory Verse

For judgement is without mercy to the one who has shown no mercy. Mercy triumphs over judgement. —James 2:13

Day Three: Faith's Work

She knew I was a Christian. When I hugged her, the smell of life on the street nearly choked me. Her life was harder than mine. She had fewer relationships, little support, and a life riddled with circumstances I could not imagine. I had walked through my share of struggles, but they were different from hers. I had a warm, safe home to sleep in. I didn't have to worry if I would eat tomorrow. I didn't have people in my life taking advantage of me at every turn. I had stood many times judging her and looking down on her missing my opportunity to love her. In this moment, shame overcame me as I realized how foolish I had been in the past. I had held thoughts about her that were unkind, assuming, and harsh. But in this moment, God was beginning to teach me to see her differently.

Like a wall, strong and prideful standing firm, when my arms wrapped around her, the wall fell down that I could have never conquered on my own. That is what God does in a heart that is willing to live full of faith. I don't tell you this because I'm proud of all the times I've failed and proud that maybe I'm starting to get it, but I tell you because I still mess up. Over and over again I have to ask God to help me to see like He wants me to. Not with eyes of judgement, but with eyes of compassion and grace. It's a daily battle.

I wish I could say faith wins every time. I don't always make the right choice. My arms don't always fall open when they should be receiving all people. I am ashamed to say that sometimes my thoughts lean toward judgment and can tend to think the worst. But, like you, I am learning day by day. Step by step, I am learning to choose to live out of my faith and exercise the mercy James teaches and Jesus shows.

Active Faith

 Take a look at this list and circle the five things you think are the most important.

Giving to the poor
Serving widows
Tithing
Teaching Bible study
Reading your Bible
Caring for orphans
Leading worship
Fasting
Cleaning the church
Giving back to the community
Praying
Picking up trash on the street
Doing yard work for the elderly

 What impacted the things you marked as important?

 If you could pick one thing from the list that you think is the most important, which one would you choose to focus on and why?

There are so many things we could do and should do as followers of Jesus. How do we know what to truly invest our time in for eternity? This is a difficult question, but if you'll dig into today's lesson with me, we will attempt to gain clarity on this perplexing question.

Was my hug a "work" to be considered faithful or an act of faith motivated by agreement with duty rather than simple love? Possibly. Or an act inspired by a love born out of faith? I think neither is sufficient to meet the goal of the gospel James speaks of in chapter 2. It's not enough to do the hugging or to check a box that I did the right deed.

It goes back to the condition of the heart and the compassion of the way we see. Looking at another person with love compels the heart to act in obedience to the nudge of the Holy Spirit's prompting. It's living each day knowing I have one chance to do the most important work of my life—be a real Christian. That means I follow Christ and I live what I say I believe. The only way to do that is by surrendering moment by moment to God's direction and following through in obedience to what He says to my heart.

Obedience to the prompting of the Holy Spirit prepares the heart to respond in faith. **This is faith in action.** It responds with the compassion of Christ. It has nothing to do with the hug or who sees or knows about the hug. **It's all about obedience to God. This is true faith.** It's an action because of the condition of a heart full of faith.

Faith is more than words. It is more than mercy. It is more than a silent feeling or compelling event. It is more than enduring many trials. Although words are heavy and hold value, faith is more than what we say. Although trials are often strengthening, faith is more than winning your battles. Faith involves living action. It's seeing and doing. It's knowing and showing up. It is more than attending a meeting. It is more than raising awareness. **Faith is the fruit of noticing, noting, and taking action. It is compassion in action whether that leads to obedient prayers of faith or obedient acts of worship.**

Digging Deeper

Faith rests on your heart's belief system. It's as if your actions mean nothing if they are not grounded and grown from a heart full of faith. The same hug I gave the girl who came from a hard place could have been given with the same arms and been obligatory, unholy, or pious. No matter how many good works we do, if they don't spring from a heart of personal faith in Jesus, and a desire to reflect the good news we know, they will not stand before the throne of God.

> **What does personal faith mean to you? Do you have religion or a personal relationship with Jesus?**

For me, personal faith takes me back to my salvation. The moment of understanding that I needed a Savior to forgive me of my sins. Without faith, I could not step forward toward a relationship with Jesus. There was an action of admitting my sin, confessing my sin, and asking Jesus to forgive me of my sin. These actions led me by faith to receive God's gift of eternal life. Is this true for you, too?

Faith is a heart belief that seeks God over a gut feeling. While faith might feel like a mustered-up, gut feeling that says, all will be well, it is so much more than that. It compels us to pray, to seek God, and to act on that prompting in our hearts to do good. It's not an idea of looking through rose-colored glasses hoping for the best. It's knowing no matter what God is good and does good, and my life is part of His plan.

Faith is obedience to God that does as God says, when God says, because God says. This applies even when all we can see is difficult circumstances. Sometimes life is so hard. That does not mean God is gone or has left us to figure out our faith. It means now is the time to start counting joy and discover how deep our faith really is rooted. Seeking God and seeing God at work is the daily practice of a believer who lives in deep faith.

Every day is a new opportunity to see who and what God has for us. Seeing and serving the people right in front of you is the lesson Jesus taught through every encounter He had. He did not see and pass by. He did not see and hope someone else would do something. He saw. He moved toward the people in front of Him. He helped. He gave hope to those who needed it.

Apply It

Loving people is good, but seeing them is the first step. This goes back to the eyes of mercy we saw yesterday. We cannot serve them unless we first see them. We pass by so quickly and we move on to the next thing on our list that we miss so many opportunities to make an impact. Life gets busy and we have an agenda. Rush here, rush there. Call them. Text back. Don't miss that activity. Get there on time. The challenge is to stop to see the faces in front of us as we rush about. When we see, we meet the need with a listening ear, words, actions, and follow-through. When we don't see, we don't serve. When we do see, we know we cannot fix everyone's problems. But it doesn't stop us from helping a new neighbor move in, noticing that a friend needs a night off, or offering to pray over someone who is upset right in the moment.

Seeing needs isn't about looking for organizations and volunteer opportunities, although those are good things. It's more about looking around your everyday life for opportunities to share what you have—the love of Jesus. It's as simple as a smile, a phone call to check in or checkup, a ride, the chance to call a stranger by name as you read off their badge at the grocery store. There are opportunities laid before us every single day because that is how the Spirit works. We get to choose awareness or ignorance, but the opportunities are there.

Needs don't wait and neither should we. It is not about showing up with a "Here I am" as you help but rather a prayer of "Lord, how can I serve this person right here?" That is faith in action. More than a feeling. More than a fleeting moment of strength. Faith is the fruit of noticing, noting, and taking action.

Prayer of Faith

Dear Lord, I want to live by faith. I don't want to just say I have faith. Help open my eyes to the needs in front of me and give me fresh eyes to see how I can act on my faith in a way that honors and glorifies You. When my faith feels weak, strengthen me to action. In Jesus' name, amen.

Memory Verse

For judgement is without mercy to the one who has shown no mercy. Mercy triumphs over judgement. —James 2:13

Day Four: Faith's History

Years ago I went on a mission trip to Japan. We would stand at the local train station and hold signs that said, "Free English practice." As the Japanese people walked by, those who knew a little English would see our signs and enter into a conversation. There was one special encounter with a dear Japanese lady that I will never forget.

Her eyes were bright with questions and her knowledge of the English language was vast. We talked about her life, her children, and eventually we began to talk about faith. Without any knowledge of God, Jesus, or the Bible, it was difficult to know where to begin.

I led with, "In the beginning God created the heavens and the earth." I continued to give a summary of the Bible as I led her through the fall of Adam and Eve and the necessary sacrifice of animals for redemption under the old covenant. This was a lot for someone with no knowledge of the Bible, but she seemed as if she wanted more so I continued to the good news of the gospel and told her what Jesus did for us. I told her of His death on the cross for all mankind and His resurrection. I explained how He is different from the gods of her country, like Buddha. I expressed to her the difference between going to a local shrine and bowing before Jesus as the One true God, alive in heaven.

She stopped me abruptly and said words of truth that are forever etched in my heart. With her wide brown eyes looking into mine, she grabbed my hand and said these words, "So to a Christian, Jesus is everything."

Yes! Somehow in my brief explanation of the Bible and the gospel, she heard the truth and understood Jesus to be the defining factor of Christianity. **The faith of a follower of Jesus resides in the fact that Jesus Christ is everything.**

Read James 2:21–24.

The faith of Abraham goes way back. I do not think James was just trying to give our forefathers a nod when he mentions Abraham. There is deep theological truth tucked within these verses as we learn about the ancient faith of Abraham. Imagine with me the scene and try to understand and comprehend the faith of Abraham. It is difficult to grasp how Abraham could take his son up the mountain knowing what God had requested of him. If you are unfamiliar with this whole story, pause for a few minutes and read Genesis 22:1–19. It's important to understand the culture of the times. Those who worshipped pagan gods in Canaan often practiced child sacrifice by allowing their children to pass through fire as a way to prove their devotion to their god.[7] The instruction God gave Abraham was proving ground for his faith and God's promises. It was a demonstration of Abraham's faith and God's faithfulness.[8] There was no need for child sacrifice when God would provide the ram.[9]

Just as God provided the ram in the place of Isaac, God provided the ultimate Lamb through His Son, Jesus. It is up to us to choose faith in Jesus. Abraham didn't have to walk up that mountain. He could have said, "Absolutely not. I won't do it!" But he had faith bigger than his fear knowing God would provide.

Digging Deeper

There are some important things we can learn about Abraham if we take a closer look. First, his father worshiped other gods. This is vital to understanding the personal nature of Abraham's faith. He grew up likely being taught to worship other gods. His faith was up to him. He could have followed what he knew, but instead he chose to follow God.

> And Joshua said to all the people, "Thus says the LORD God of Israel: 'Your fathers, including Terah, the father of Abraham and the father of Nahor, dwelt on the other side of the River in old times; and they served other gods.'" —Joshua 24:2

Read Genesis 12:1–4. How old was Abraham when God instructed him to go and promised him a blessing?

Abraham was up in years when God first spoke to him and told him to take action. This gives us some truth about God we must not miss. God is not partial to age. He is not only looking to bless and speak to young people who have their entire lives ahead of them. He is always working in every life throughout the span of life to bless and call all men to Himself.

Your faith, no matter how old or young, can be active and alive. You don't have to wonder if it's too late. You don't have to be defeated thinking you've messed up too many times. You have time because you have today. There has never been a better day to prove your faith than right now.

Let's turn our attention toward Isaac for just a minute. I wonder what he thought? I wonder if he looked around planning an escape? I wonder if he imagined rolling off the altar at the last minute just before the knife came down. We don't get a whole lot from the dialogue between him and Abraham, but we get enough to know he did question Abraham. But it seems Abraham's response to Isaac satisfied Isaac's question(s). He laid down on the altar. Even watched as his dad lifted the knife over his body. Isaac's faith is also worth noticing.

Not only did Abraham have an intimate relationship with God so much that he took this unbelievable step of obedience, it seems Isaac also relied heavily on either his father's leadership or on God's. The faith we see here is deep faith in action. They said, "I love God so much, I will do what He says no matter what, even when I cannot understand." They each and both trusted God. Their actions proved that God was everything.

The faith they exhibited was not a result of work they had done. It was the obedient action they took to walk up the mountain and prepare to make the sacrifice that proved their faith. Their works flowed from their faith. Their work did not produce faith, but it did increase the faith they already had. The natural progression of faith increases as we take steps of obedience to God's instruction. Abraham's obedience by faith in God resulted in God's blessing, which in turn increased not only Abraham's faith, but also his son Isaac's faith.

Apply It

When I think about my own faith, I would love to say I have faith like Abraham. But sadly, I often hold on so tightly to things in my life especially when it comes to people I love.

When my first daughter got her driver's license, my heart seemed to hit my throat and lodge there. The thought of her going out on the road in a vehicle terrified me. It brought visions of emergency rooms, life flights, and funerals that I didn't want to walk through. Fear paralyzes me sometimes. While it's a possibility that my daughter could get into an accident, there is also the very real possibility that she won't. Only God knows. At some point, I had to peel my hands off the idea that I could control the outcome of any trip she took in the car. I had to remind myself no matter what happens, Jesus is everything.

We can let fear grip our faith so tightly that it literally chokes it out. It happens so easily. That is when we are on proving ground: Is Jesus everything or not? Faith in action says, "I trust God even though I cannot control it, fix it, understand, see, or do anything about it. God will provide. He always does. He always has."

He did for Abraham. He will for me. It does not mean that bad things will never happen or that life won't throw curve balls that hit you from out of nowhere. It means God's plan is bigger, and sometimes He allows difficult things that will prove the strength of our faith.

Read the following verses and look for one thing each of these verses has in common. To make it easy, circle the word "friend" in each verse. Underline the name "Abraham" in each verse.

 "Are **You not our God,** *who* **drove out the inhabitants of this land before Your people Israel, and gave it to the descendants of Abraham Your friend forever?" (2 Chronicles 20:7)**

 "But you, Israel, *are* **My servant, Jacob whom I have chosen, The descendants of Abraham My friend." (Isaiah 41:8)**

> And the Scripture was fulfilled which says, "Abraham believed God, and it was accounted to him for righteousness." And he was called the friend of God. —James 2:23

Multiple times throughout Scripture Abraham is referred to as "the friend of God." I have heard songs that call God our friend, and I have read articles that talk about God as our friend. In Proverbs 18:24, Solomon says, "A man *who has* friends must himself be friendly, But there is a friend *who* sticks closer than a brother." This comparison is referring to the potential of an intimate relationship with God.

In Genesis 15:4–5, God promised Abraham he would have so many descendants that they would be in more number than the stars. Not only that, but that those offspring would come from his own son. His only son was Isaac. Abraham trusted God's promise as he led Isaac up the mountain and He believed God would follow through on His promise.

 Read Hebrews 11:17–19. How was Abraham's faith proven?

Sometimes God's ways don't seem fair. It is difficult to understand why God would want us to give up certain things or go places that don't seem comfortable. But just as God made provision for Abraham; God always has a plan and a promise for us, too. His promises through His Word give us something to cling to when we don't understand. One of my favorite places to go in Scripture when life seems unfair is Proverbs 3:5–6 that says, "Trust in the LORD with all your heart, And lean not on your own understanding; In all your ways acknowledge Him, And He shall direct your paths."

We might not always understand, but we can stand on the proven ground of our faith and hold on to the One who does understand. This is where we get to decide if our faith will override our fears or if we will buckle beneath the weight of worldly wisdom and reasoning. Abraham had every reason not to take his son up the mountain, but he also had every reason to because of what he believed about his God. Let God's promises lead your faith to work and when you start wondering how everything will work out, remind yourself of this truth—to a Christian, Jesus is everything.

Prayer of Faith

Dear Lord, I want to have faith that works. Not for my good, but because You are good. Thank You for giving me faith to get this far in my life. Increase my faith as I continually learn to follow You through the ups and downs of life. Help me remember You are everything. In Jesus' name, amen.

Memory Verse

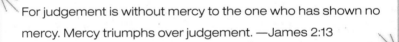

For judgement is without mercy to the one who has shown no mercy. Mercy triumphs over judgement. —James 2:13

Day Five: Faith's Redemption

It was the early morning hours of the day. No one was awake. When the phone rang, I knew. We had been walking the halls of the hospital for about four months. The day before, I had sat a long time with Dad. I played songs of comfort on my phone as we sat in the stillness of my dad's breathing. His breathing had changed over the past weeks, and we knew his life would transfer to heaven any moment. Even though we knew, we weren't prepared. I don't know if you can ever truly prepare for losing a loved one.

We were not gathered around his bedside. We were not watching him take his last breath. We had said good night and deep into the night in the early morning, Jesus took him home to heaven.

We walked into the hospital. It was the same route we walked each day. We rode the elevator up to the fourth floor and took a right, then a left. We passed the rooms of others who were ill and reaching the end of life. Then we stopped at Dad's room and walked in for the last time.

When we entered the room immediately it felt differently than it had all those months before. Dad lay there with no breath, and we stood, our breath seemingly taken away, too. And then the words came without a thought, "He's not here."

And he wasn't. Although his body was there, his spirit was not present in that hospital room.

I will never read James 2:26 the same after that experience. *For as the body without the spirit is dead, so faith without works is dead also.* Just as my dad was not present in the hospital room, faith is not present without action. Without work there is no faith. To pretend like there is, is like a dead body laying there as if it is alive. It's impossible. The chest doesn't rise and fall with each breath. The blood does not flow. The hands and the feet don't work. There is no brain power to fuel activity. There is no pulse to show signs of life. And the color begins to dim. It is literally breathtaking, stripping the body of all it needs. This is what inaction does to faith. It strips it of its power.

Faith in action is a power that the enemy cannot compete with. Show me a woman in Christ who holds faith like it is her life, and I'll show you a woman who can walk through the fire and storms of life every single time no matter how hard it gets. Show me a woman who thinks God owes her the world and sits back waiting for God to bless her, and I'll show you a girl who is like a dead corpse wishing it could somehow take a deep breath. True faith is alive and active. And sometimes that faith is put to the test. It took Rahab being forced with a faith decision to prove her faith. She had every excuse to lean into her heartache, sin, and baggage and resist the spies, but instead she moved with faith toward what she knew was right and her faith is forever note-worthy because of it.

Digging Deeper

Faith is not reserved for the elite. It is reserved for the alive. If you have breath, you have the opportunity to live in deep faith. It is not too late. We find this fact true for the woman named Rahab that James mentions. James says her actions of taking in the spies proved her faith. It justified her even though she had a sinful past. This is just one example of the ways God gives opportunities for people to come to Him.

> By faith the harlot Rahab did not perish with those who did not believe, when she had received the spies with peace.
> —Hebrews 11:31

Even though Rahab lived a sinful life as a prostitute, when she encountered God's people, she proved her faith in God with her actions and God saved her life. Stories like this are hard to grasp. She had both condemnable and commendable actions. She lived a life that would have been openly awful, yet God used her in multiple ways to shine for Him. Her name lives on in the "hall of faith" in Hebrews and here in James as someone who rose above the potential ashes of her life and proved faithful with a split-second decision. The difference for Rahab was in what she had heard and believed along the way and then the action she took because of what she believed. The seeds of faith planted in her heart took root, and in a moment of decision, she acted on what she believed by taking in the spies and protecting God's people.

This gives us great hope. God can use you. No matter how dirty or messed up your life may be, God can use your life to bring Him glory and accomplish His purpose. When we know the truth and act on the truth we know, that is faith in action. The action does not save us, but the action proves what is on the inside. If Rahab would have turned the men away or had exposed them, her faith would have been proven to be weak and insufficient. Even after hearing that God parted the Red Sea, in her heart it would have proved she didn't believe God could protect this time. But in her heart, her faith told her God could and would, therefore she did what she knew was right in that moment. Her faith shined and still shines today.

The roots of our faith are developed in the quiet moments of hearing God's Word, and the fruit is produced in the steps we take to obey God's Word. This is what Paul speaks of in Romans 10:16–17 when he says, "But they have not all obeyed the gospel. For Isaiah says, 'LORD, who has believed our report?' So then faith *comes* by hearing, and hearing by the word of God." Rahab had heard the truth, but it took a forced moment of decision for her to act on what her heart already knew.

There is one more thing about Rahab that is worth noting. If we investigate her family tree, we find two things that show us how God redeems broken lives and brings about beauty from brokenness.

 Read Ruth 2:10–12. Why did Boaz have compassion for Ruth according to these verses?

Boaz had compassion for Ruth and redeemed Ruth's story from widowhood to wife because of her actions of faith to help Naomi. Of course we know God orchestrated every detail. But Ruth's faith made her even more noteworthy to Boaz. This is important because Boaz was the son of Rahab the harlot.

Not only did Rahab's family line include the beautiful story of Ruth, but if we look into generations listed in Matthew 1:5–16, we discover Jesus came through the family line of Rahab.

Only God could connect the dots like this. Do not assume life is just a myriad of odd circumstances. God has a plan bigger than any of us that leads us to Him and His glory. **Let your faith work and believe God is able to redeem the most broken and make it the most beautiful.**

Apply It

Think about the seeds of faith that have been planted in your heart throughout your life. Consider the times you've heard sermons preached, testimonies given, stories of God's miracles, or seen lives changed. Maybe a song spoke the exact words you needed, or an encounter with a stranger was the help you needed in the moment. Have you experienced moments when you know God was planting seeds of faith in your heart because of what you have heard or learned about Him and what He has done? These moments mark our hearts and we have the responsibility to lean into them or ignore the message God is giving us.

How does knowing what God is capable of increase your capacity for deeper faith?

If faith and actions work together, what is one thing you can do to exercise or strengthen your faith muscles?

When you think about faith that is dead, what does that look like to you?

In contrast, what does active faith life look like to you? How can you live with increasing faith that is alive?

Prayer of Faith

Dear Lord, I want to be an active faithful follower of Christ. I don't want to be found thinking about my faith so much that I'm missing out on acting on it. I want to live with faith and move forward in faith so much that there is no chance for the enemy to get a foothold in my life. In Jesus' name, amen.

Memory Verse

For judgement is without mercy to the one who has shown no mercy. Mercy triumphs over judgement. —James 2:13

Full of Faith When Your Heart Is Tested

Day One: Faith's Voice

It's time to open your Bible or Bible app and read James chapters 3 and 4. Don't skip this important step of our time together. It will help lay the foundation and offer a fuller understanding of what is coming up this week.

"You are crazy." Her words didn't mean to hurt me but they did. She was a Christian lady. She was the type of lady that makes people casseroles and does nice things for others when they need help. But her words hit a tender place in my heart.

It was true. I felt crazy sometimes. The life our family lives does look a little different than some. With cram-packed schedules, a home exploding with children, extra-large vehicles to accommodate our always expanding family due to foster care, and endless trips to the grocery store, we live a life that is super full. As foster parents it means at any moment I might not be able to tell you how many children I actually have. Some days it's four, other days it's five or six or maybe seven. If we are at a restaurant, please don't make me tell the lady at the front how many seats or highchairs we need. I might not be able to remember and it might send me into a panic thinking we've forgotten someone somewhere. Ha! So, yes. Maybe I actually am a little on the crazy side. The question, "Who has the baby?" has been asked about a thousand times. "Which baby?" is the response most recently as we have three babies under two years old. Crazy? Probably. But exactly where God wants us. Crazy and all.

Many people spoke kind words to me that particular week. But the words that stuck with me and replayed over and over in my head as I changed diapers, wiped mouths, and had long talks with my teenagers about stuff no one ever prepared me for were hers: "You. Are. Crazy."

Think back to the last time someone said something to you that hurt your heart. Now, think about when you last received a compliment. If you are anything like me, there can be one hundred compliments, but it's usually the criticism that sticks. Maybe this is why James used almost an entire chapter to talk about our words and the connection they have to our faith.

When we use our words carelessly, the enemy is meticulously and maliciously articulating them to damage the body of Christ. I know she didn't really mean I was actually crazy. She just meant, "Wow, honey! You've got a lot on your plate." But that is not what she said. The enemy used her words to hurt and sting my heart in a deep way. An innocent comment made an internal connection to my heart.

The words we say matter.

Whether it's the words you say to yourself in your head or the words that come out of your actual mouth, they are heavy and make an impact wherever they land. They hold a key to the thoughts of the heart and prove what is deep inside. The words come from either a place of reverence and fear of God steeped in deep faith or from a shallow pool of thoughtlessness that oozes and gushes wherever they may. If your words are filled with hope and encouragement, your heart is probably seeking and seeing the good things God is doing.

When faith is the foundation of your words, the fruit of them is beautiful. On the other hand, careless words that pop out in the heat of the moment, or spew forth before you think, or tumble and fumble without warning, those words potentially wind up bearing painful fruit.

There is one clear way to tell who is full of faith and who isn't. If you pay close attention for even a little bit, you'll be able to pick out the people who live with strong faith and those who waiver and wobble and wonder if God will work everything out. Words show a lot about a person's foundation of faith. It's an indicator of what's going around and around in the heart and mind. People who live in a deep place of reverential fear of God typically live with words that flow with faith and sweet fruit.

The tongue is not just a little thing that helps us know if our food is too spicy or if our tea is sweet enough. It's a weapon that has the potential to impact others with wounds, worry, and waste. It can also work like a balm, soothing the deepest hurt and settling the struggling soul. The strong desire to use your words as a healing agent rather than an irritant is the fear necessary to control the wild beast we hold of our words.

In Proverbs 9:10 we find the phrase, "the fear of the LORD." If we study Scripture we will find it multiple places, but it can often be skipped over or misunderstood. What if I said it is ok to have fear in your heart? The fear we want to hold in our hearts is not the kind that makes us terrified when we hear a noise in the night or makes the heart beat hard when danger is near. Healthy fear of the heart is the kind that keeps you from saying unkind words and makes you think before you blurt out exactly what you really think. It's a strong reverence and surrender to our Holy God who helps tame your tongue. This is one of the only ways to reign in the words you say. Words must be tamed. Like a dog has to learn to come, sit, and rollover, the tongue must learn when to speak, when to stop, and when to shut up. It's not something I'm always great at, but I am constantly learning and growing. I know you are, too.

When the soul is tested, what is deep within will emerge through our words. For in the words we speak, we see a glimpse into the heart. If you listen, you'll hear a person's heart through not only their words, but their works.

Think of something that makes you feel like you need to make a difference, do something, take action, or advocate. What makes you feel like you have to say something and cannot keep quiet? What makes you angry to the point of speaking up? Or gets your heart beating to the point of taking a step forward? That thing is usually close to your heart. When the heart gets bumped, whatever is deep inside comes out. It's the things that you feel passionate about. It might be as simple as what kind of shampoo you prefer or how to eat an Oreo. Or as complex as how you feel about politics, religion, or the family unit and what love really means.

For me, it's things like foster care, family, faith, and even my failures. I get so consumed with how I can make a difference in the world that I have to share with others what God is doing in my heart. I sometimes wonder if others feel as passionately as I do about the same things in their lives. Then I listen. And I hear it. For some, their passion flows from their job, their home, their hobbies, or even how they utilize every hour of the day. At times passion is even for the things we don't have. We wonder why we don't have children, or haven't gotten promoted, or haven't found the perfect husband. We wait for life to work out, but we get busy talking about what everyone else has and what we wish we had. Days get filled up fast with scrolling and scolding the world for their foolish ways and yet here we are wondering why our faith feels weak.

Feeling weak in testing isn't because we don't know what to say. It's because we've filled our hearts with the wrong kind of fear. We talk about all the things we don't have, and forget the one thing we should have. The fear of God brings great wisdom to the words we say. Rather than, "You are crazy" to the lady who is just trying to follow God's will for her life, we will see her efforts in a different light.

A more faith-filled choice of words might be, "I think it's awesome how you embrace exactly what God has for your life." Doesn't that touch the heart in a beautiful way? But these words only come from a foundation of faith. When the heart is filled with the ways of the world, the ways of the world will roll right off the tongue. Fearing God and seeing through eyes of faith brings a new light to the way we see others and the words we say.

Digging Deeper

 In James 3:6, what is the tongue compared to?

Fire isn't bad when it is under control, but when it is running rampant and has no boundaries or attention, it is dangerous and destructive. It can take over a home, field, or city in a short amount of time.

But when fire is under control it can be a blessing. It can offer warmth on a cold winter night. One of my favorite ways to utilize a fire is by putting a marshmallow on a stick and holding it over the fire for just a moment to soften that fluffy white sugar up until it's brown on the edges and soft on the inside. That is a blessed marshmallow. But if you hold the marshmallow over the fire too long, it gets burned and charred and eventually unusable. This is the same with our words. They can be helpful and so good, or they can be destructive and ridiculously useless leaving only a sad memory.

 How can a fire be a blessing or a help?

 How can a fire ruin what it comes in contact with?

 In Proverbs 12:18 we find two different types of people.

- A person who speaks like a piercing sword
- A person who speaks wisely and promotes health

There is an interesting fact mentioned in this proverb: **Wise words are good for your health.**

Have you ever wondered why you feel better after listening to someone who seems to be filled with wisdom? This is why. "Sticks and stones may break my bones, but words will never hurt" is a myth. It's a lie from the enemy to undermine God's truth. Words matter so much.

Think for a moment about how God used His words in the Bible stories we know. God *spoke* the world into existence in Genesis. Jesus healed several times by simply *speaking* to individuals throughout Matthew, Mark, Luke, and John. Jesus calmed the sea with *His words*. Jesus *taught* the people and pointed people to God the Father so that they might know Him. While we won't be able to create or heal like God did with our words, we do have the power to use our words for good and godliness. And through our words, God will impact the lives of others. We hold a great responsibility to steward our words well.

 In Proverbs 15:14, we find two different types of people. Beyond that, we find what they seek or feed on. I have listed the two types of people for you. Fill in beside each one what the Bible says to describe them.

    1. The person who has a heart of understanding—They seek _____

    2. The person who has a foolish mouth—They feed on _____

This is where training the mouth comes full circle. The foolish mouth feeds on foolishness. The understanding mouth feeds on and seeks out knowledge. It's a choice to learn God's Word or the ways of the world.

We can feast on information all day long. It's everywhere. With the tap of our thumb on a smartphone or the word of our mouth to a device we can get information at any moment. If we neglect God's Word, we will never begin to tame the tip of the tongue. It is God's Word that gives us the information and transformation we need to use our words for good. **Taming the tongue isn't for the faint of heart. It's for the faithful heart.**

Apply It

 Name one time when words have hurt your heart.

I know you probably have more than one, but the goal is not to bring up every hurt. The goal is to evaluate how words prove our faith. If you have been hurt by words, you know that the person offering the painful words must have some pain themselves tied up in their hearts. Out of the treasure of the heart is where those words came from. Rather than getting angry again over the words spoken to you, evaluate how you can pray for the person who hurt you.

 Name one time when you have hurt someone with your words.

Sometimes we say things without thinking. Today let's stop and think. No matter how old we are, we have an opportunity to continue to tame the weapon of the tongue, but we need help. The only way to be successful in this effort is to fill our hearts full of faith. It looks a lot like filling up on the Word of God and leaning into the healthy reverence to our Almighty God.

 Identify one person you can encourage with your words today. Send them a text or card and use your words for good.

Prayer of Faith

Dear Lord, forgive me for the times I have used my words to hurt and not heal. Help me fill my heart with God's Word so good things flow out of my mouth. Guide my thoughts and my heart to speak of things that would help others and honor You. In Jesus' name, amen.

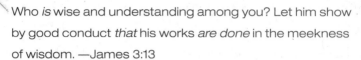

Memory Verse

Who *is* wise and understanding among you? Let him show by good conduct *that* his works *are done* in the meekness of wisdom. —James 3:13

Day Two: Faith's Place

Testing comes in many forms. Sometimes it is sickness that draws us to our knees. Other times it is financial struggles that leave us begging God for help and provision. Then there are relationship struggles that make us wonder if we can push through and get along. But when testing comes because someone we thought was close to God fails us with hurtful words or actions, it is difficult to resolve the wounds inflicted on the heart. Maybe you don't have the same experience with church that I have had in my life. But I can tell you from *my* experience I have watched church people get up on Sunday to sing, preach, pray, or teach the Bible, only to step into Monday and wound the hearts of others deeply.

It began in my early years when my dad who was a pastor left our family and our church. My faith was tested, and I was forced to figure out if my faith was connected to my father or my personal relationship with Jesus. It took me years to sort it all out, but eventually I had to make the decision that my faith was not tied to a person on this earth but only to the one person who died for my sins—Jesus Christ. When we realize this truth, our faith can move beyond the wounds and words of others. When we forget this truth, we will live captive to the failures of men and women who hurt us. Especially if those wounds happen within the walls of our place of worship.

Before we go any farther, let me be clear that I love the church. I have grown up in church, and I live my life to serve my Savior specifically in the church. My husband has always worked in the church, and it is not only our livelihood but the joy of our lives to serve the people God has put us with. That being said, there were days in the past when my heart was deeply scarred by the church. I have talked with enough women over the years to know that many of us have experienced some pain inside the walls of a place we would love to call a safe space of church.

If your heart has been wounded within the place of faith, rather than let it make you bitter toward church, let it make you better. I can testify of God's amazing grace to make me a better woman because of the bitter life experience I have endured. Every experience in life we go through has the potential to make us a better person or a worse person. We can learn from what we go through and grow through it. Or we can let what we go through infest us, making us a living cancer that sits in a pew with every reason in the world to be angry and negative about church. Or worse, never step foot in church again. This is exactly what the devil wants. He would love to get you so wrapped up in the evil someone else has done that it ignites the evil within your heart to hate God and the people who proclaim His truth.

Here is a life lesson that will help all of us:

- People will fail.
- They do.
- I do.
- We all do.
- But God.
- He never fails.

The church is not a place for perfect people to gather and worship God. It is a place for messed up people like **you and me** to worship a perfect God. Did you catch that? You and me. We are not perfect. If people were perfect, there would be no need for God or Jesus or salvation. Do not allow the failure of someone else or your own failure keep you from rising back up and serving God.

You can rise above what someone else has done to you, or what someone else has said about you, or the sin someone else has gotten wrapped up in.

You can repent and come back to the God you know loves you no matter what.

You can receive forgiveness and restoration even now.

You can serve God even when your heart hurts over sin.

There's never been a better time to let God into your mess than when you feel so wounded, so worried, so wound up over all you have been through.

If we don't turn to God when we are wounded, we will end up wounding others. We will live exactly like the people James is speaking to. James' audience tried to use their words to both bless and curse. This is a direct result of attempting to live a life of wounded faith. Whether those wounds are self-inflicted by your own sin or unprovoked trauma from someone else's sin, when faith is wounded it must be cared for carefully and diligently.

This is where we must get to work. Will you stay down and lick your wounds or let God heal them with His truth? Let's see how James can help us discern how to move from wounded by those in the church to a place of deep faith in spite of the sin.

Digging Deeper

Does a spring send forth fresh *water* and bitter from the same opening? Can a fig tree, my brethren, bear olives, or a grapevine bear figs? Thus no spring yields both salt water and fresh. —James 3:11–12

There is a strong contrast we notice in James 3:11–12 to define the difference between faith-filled words that help and heal and foolish words that hurt and steal. Look at each contrasting word James uses to describe our words and notice how they are opposite. Circle the positive word in each pair.

- Blessing / cursing
- Fresh water / bitter water
- Salt water / fresh water

Imagine you have a multiple-choice question on a test. You cannot choose A and B. It cannot be both. There is no "all of the above choice" on the test. It is either A or B. If you try to choose both, the question is marked incorrect. It is the same with our words. We cannot try to bless people on Sunday and curse and criticize them Monday through Friday. It does not add up and it does not please God. While we might think this is obvious, there is a reason this strong instruction about words is here.

The church can be a social place of words that spread like wildfire. Think of the last big sin you heard about. Who told you? How many people knew before them? What did you do with the information? It's difficult to admit that we seem to like to hold and share information about others. But I've been there in the conversations where the latest gossip is spreading and my flesh wants to know more and more and more. I don't know why, but it's in our flesh to find out the details. Who else was there? Who else knows? How did it happen? Where did they do it? Will they be punished? And on and on our minds search for more information about something we don't even need to know.

Gossip isn't new to the modern church. It was a problem that dates all the way back to Adam and Eve. Remember what Adam did when God confronted his sin. He blamed Eve. He gossiped about her that she made him fail. That does not give us an excuse to keep gossiping, but rather it should give us a clear example of what not to do and why. The words we say impact our faith positively or negatively. More than that, the words we share show our faith whether it be positive or negative. The words we say can impact other believers for growth or for doubt. Our words tell the world whether we are growing with deep roots or being scorched by the sun. Eventually the results will show the condition of the heart. Dry and crispy without life or flourishing and full like one that is close to the river receiving all it needs to flourish. The choice is completely up to us.

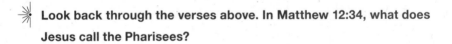 **Jesus has some strong words to say about the words we say in Matthew 12. Read these verses and mark every place you see a word that implies the idea of bad or evil.**

"Either make the tree good and its fruit good, or else make the tree bad and *its* fruit bad; for a tree is known by its fruit. Brood of vipers! How can you, being evil, speak good things? For out of the abundance of the heart the mouth speaks. A good man out of the good treasure of his heart brings forth good things, and an evil man out of the evil treasure brings forth evil things. But I say to you that for every idle word men may speak, they will give account of it in the day of judgment. For by your words you will be justified, and by your words you will be condemned."
—Matthew 12:33–37

Look back through the verses above. In Matthew 12:34, what does Jesus call the Pharisees?

The word picture here couldn't get any clearer. Like a pit of snakes, those who say one thing and do another are just waiting with the other snakes ready to destroy others. It's sickening when you think of the reality. Yet it happens, and you could probably tell stories of it in your life. But here we have an opportunity to make a difference. Do not be a snake! Instead, be like good fruit. Sweet and satisfying. This means we don't talk behind others' backs. We don't back bite. We don't spread gossip or the latest news on the street. Instead encourage. Lift up. Be a truth teller and be known as one who shuts down the telephone game and doesn't get involved with the stuff that hurts unless it directly involves you.

Apply It

> Anxiety in the heart of man causes depression, But a good word makes it glad. —Proverbs 12:25

According to Proverbs 12:25, the result of anxiety is _____. The result of a good word is _____.

Identify a time when you were unfaithful with your words. For me this looks like speaking too harshly, being short, or even holding back my words because I think I'm right. Pride is usually a factor in my failure in this area. It is worse when I feel like I am being attacked or tested. I feel the need to prove myself. What about you?

How can you use your words to help?

Identify specific people you want to impact with healthy words? Maybe it's a co-worker, family member, friend, church member, or neighbor.

> Pleasant words are like a honeycomb, sweetness to the soul and health to the bones. —Proverbs 16:24

Prayer of Faith

Dear Lord, I do not want to live in the land of both blessing and cursing. I want to speak words that will soothe and comfort and bless others. When I am tempted to lash out, exaggerate, cut down, or prove something, remind me to prove my faith by my words. In Jesus' name, amen.

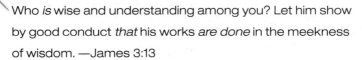

Memory Verse

Who *is* wise and understanding among you? Let him show by good conduct *that* his works *are done* in the meekness of wisdom. —James 3:13

Day Three: Faith's Peace

We are going to begin today with a question. Think about the wisest person you know. Maybe it is a parent or a mentor. Perhaps a teacher or a coach. Or maybe you have a pastor or a leader you admire that seems to ooze with wisdom every time they speak. Think about the person that comes to mind. For me, I'm thinking of a pastor who is still preaching into his nineties. For one, I think it's amazing that he is still using his gift and calling, but also every time I hear him speak it feels as if God is speaking directly through him to my heart. He radiates God's wisdom.

Today's question: Who is it for you? Think about this person and what makes them different from other people in your life.

 What makes this person wise?

Maybe your answer is quick and easy or maybe you have to think hard and evaluate what true wisdom really means. For me, wise people are people who know God's peace deeply. They've walked through fire, storms, death, and devastating circumstances yet still hold God's peace tightly in their hearts. Their lives preach a message they couldn't say in words. Which brings us to an interesting contrast to James 3. How our words and wisdom interact, prove our faith. They show who we are on the inside.

Today's Scripture tells us the fruit of true faith is wisdom in action which leads to peace. Isn't that what we all want? Peace? As we talk about peace, let's take a little quiz.

The Peace Quiz

Instructions: Do not linger on each question. Quickly choose your answer and move to the next question. Ready? Get set. Go!

 How do you feel when you get bad news?

    A. It doesn't bother me.

    B. I freeze as I try to absorb what I've just heard.

    C. I panic and start trying to make plans to fix it.

    D. I run and avoid reality.

 What goes through your head when you cannot get ahold of someone you love?

    A. They are fine.

    B. Maybe they got in an accident.

    C. They have been abducted.

    D. They are avoiding me.

 How many times do you check the door locks at night before you go to bed?

    A. None

    B. 1

    C. 2–5

    D. More than 5

Do you second guess yourself about turning off the curling iron, straightener, or toaster?

  A. Never

  B. Sometimes

  C. Every day

  D. More than once a day

 Do you worry about what people think of you?

  A. Never

  B. Sometimes

  C. Most of the time

  D. I lay in bed at night and replay the day and wonder what they think.

 Are you concerned if someone looks at you with a bad look on their face?

  A. Absolutely not

  B. It bothers me a little.

  C. It goes all over me and makes me want to know what they are thinking.

  D. I memorize their face and can't get it out of my head.

 Do you google your symptoms when you or someone you love has an unusual headache?

  A. No, you can't believe everything on the internet.

  B. Sometimes

  C. Doesn't everyone?

  D. I can self-diagnose most illnesses because I've self-educated myself through google.

While you might chuckle at some of the questions or swallow hard because anxiety grips you at the thought of some of these. It's important we think about what causes anxiety, which in turn steals our peace. Often what people say, how they say it, and what they don't say all play into how peaceful we feel. If you are anything like me, you know what it's like to worry, wonder, and imagine the worst about yourself, your future, and what others might say or think. It doesn't help when health concerns complicate things or when bad things actually do happen to us. Even more so, anxiety rises and peace feels distant.

I'm ashamed to say I've planned unnecessary funerals of my husband or family whom I couldn't reach by text or call fast enough. I begin to think the worst and imagine they have gotten into a terrible car accident. I play out the entire thing in my head. Like a scary movie, I imagine getting the phone call or a police officer coming to my door to tell me my loved one passed away. It's terrible to bury someone who is still alive over and over.

I've imagined going in to kiss my child goodnight only to find them lifeless and not breathing. Yet my child is perfectly healthy and sound asleep. I have wondered if my mother was lying unconscious in her home when she wouldn't answer her phone. In reality she was just outside and didn't happen to take her phone with her. Those thoughts that run through our minds steal our peace.

Sometimes there are real life circumstances like illness, financial strain, relationships that are teetering on breaking, and other factors that cause what feels like unbearable stress. For me, it's things like the cancer diagnosis that touched both Rob's dad and mine too close together. It's the difficult past that comes with the foster children we love. It's the mean things people say or do that make me wonder if they even know or care about the real me.

We could all make a big list of the things that snatch our peace. But rather than dwelling on that, let's instead take a look at the opposite of what steals our peace and grasp tightly to the thing that will offer us peace in the place of anxiety. There's a word James gives us that is the pathway to peace—it is *wisdom*.

Before we can seek out wisdom and expect to get peace, we have to believe peace is possible. There is a verse that helps me remember not only the possibility of peace, but the promise of it. It's found in John 14:27. "Peace I leave with you, My peace I give to you; not as the world gives do I give to you. Let not your heart be troubled, neither let it be afraid."

I love this verse about peace because it tells us peace and fear work in the opposite directions of one another. With fear, my faith is oppressed and attacked. With peace, my faith is proven. Fear and peace are polar opposites working against each other. In order to get to peace, we've got to put fear in its rightful place.

Let's break it down the way James does and see what we can discover. Fear walks with anxiety and offers questions of doubt, uncertainty, and stress. Peace walks with faith and offers calm, assurance, and strength. If we want to have peace, we have to walk in faith. If we want to have faith, we have to walk in wisdom. It's a journey of knowing what is true and receiving truth. It's choosing to believe peace can rule in our hearts because of faith. It's not just knowing peace is possible, it's knowing it is possible for me. When you know peace is available to you, but you do not know how to access it, you will continue to live in fear. Anxiety will grip you until you can't move, and fear will tell you lies you will believe.

Peace speaks, too. But the wisdom peace shares fights the fears in your head. It's a fighting match between what you see and what you believe.

Though life might look and feel out of control, the wisdom of peace says, God is in complete control. Though your heart might feel wounded and worried, the wisdom of peace says, God is able to heal and make whole. Wisdom is not withheld for the ones who hurt the most or live life perfectly. **Wisdom is a gift from God to those who ask for it.**

Digging Deeper

James uses several words to describe wisdom from above or wisdom from God. I find it interesting these descriptive words are on the heels of

His teaching all about our words. It's as if our words ought to have these qualities and our speech ought to drip with the dignity of wisdom. Wow! Sounds powerful when we say it that way, doesn't it?

Take a look at each of these words we find in James 3:17 and define the word in your own terms. Then read the supporting Scripture for each word. Evaluate yourself to determine if your heart and words exhibit these character qualities.

But the wisdom that is from above is first pure, then peaceable, gentle, willing to yield, full of mercy and good fruits, without partiality and without hypocrisy. —James 3:17

Pure

Every word of God *is* pure; He *is* a shield to those who put their trust in Him. —Proverbs 30:5

Peaceable

And the peace of God, which surpasses all understanding, will guard your hearts and minds through Christ Jesus. —Philippians 4:7

Gentle

A soft answer turns away wrath, But a harsh word stirs up anger. The tongue of the wise uses knowledge rightly, But the mouth of fools pours forth foolishness. —Proverbs 15:1–2

Willing to yield

So then, my beloved brethren, let every man be swift to hear, slow to speak, slow to wrath. —James 1:19

Full of mercy

For judgment is without mercy to the one who has shown no mercy. Mercy triumphs over judgment. —James 2:13

Full of good fruit

Every tree that does not bear good fruit is cut down and thrown into the fire. Therefore by their fruits you will know them. —Matthew 7:19–20

Without partiality

For there is no partiality with God. —Romans 2:11

Without hypocrisy

"But woe to you, scribes and Pharisees, hypocrites! For you shut up the kingdom of heaven against men; for you neither go in *yourselves*, nor do you allow those who are entering to go in. Woe to you, scribes and Pharisees, hypocrites! For you devour widows' houses, and for a pretense make long prayers. Therefore you will receive greater condemnation. Woe to you, scribes and Pharisees, hypocrites! For you travel land and sea to win one proselyte, and when he is won, you make him twice as much a son of hell as yourselves." —Matthew 23:13–15

Apply It

We could say that wise words work wonders when it comes to peace in our lives. Paul knew the secret to peace. He told the Philippian church not to be anxious about anything, but rather ask God.[1] James knew the secret, too. The secret to peace is wise faith which produces wise words.

When we live an unwise life, our faith suffers and therefore our peace suffers. Wisdom from God gives us what we need when our faith is tested, but we have to be willing to receive peace. Too often we wrestle, kick, and scream to get what we think we want only to end up discouraged, doubting, and more anxious than when we started.

Wise living doesn't come by holding on for dear life, it comes by letting go of everything and letting God direct our lives. That's wisdom in action. That's deep faith. It says, "I choose to let God have His way, in His time, in His wisdom because I know He is able, all-knowing, all-powerful, and ready to fight for me no matter how hard life in front of me seems." Therefore I choose to let go in faith. The result is perfect peace.

 What in your life do you need to let go so that you can live a wise life? Maybe it's thoughts that steal your peace or cause constant anxiety. Write down the things God is prompting your heart to let go.

Prayer of Faith

Dear Lord, I want to live a life of peace. But I know it cannot be so without me first asking You for wisdom. I trust You know best and You do best. Today I am letting go and leaning into the faith I know will give me peace. In Jesus' name, amen.

Memory Verse

Who *is* wise and understanding among you? Let him show by good conduct *that* his works *are done* in the meekness of wisdom. —James 3:13

Day Four: Faith's Humility

The call came at the most unexpected time. I knew deep in my bones God was telling us to say, yes! So, I lifted the phone from my ear and told Rob. "They have a healthy two-week-old baby that they can't find a home for."

I wish I could describe the look on his face. It was shock, fear, and confidence all wrapped up in a man who had chosen to somehow lead our family through this unconventional life. I told the social worker I would call right back. Rob and I talked briefly about how ridiculous it seemed to add another baby to our crew. We had recently moved and were in the middle of renovations, but we knew God was saying yes. I called the social worker back without knowing anything about the baby and said, "We'll take him!" Before we hung up the phone, I asked, "What is his name?" For his privacy we will call him Baby Jay.

I quickly gathered my purse and headed to the store to get all the baby things we needed for Baby Jay. We didn't have a plan of where he would sleep or how I would possibly have the energy to love him. And I wondered if he would receive my love.

As I pulled into the Department of Children's Services a sweet peace fell over me. I stepped into the office toward a car seat that held a precious new baby and a lady holding a trash bag full of Baby Jay's belongings. I signed a piece of paper and walked out the door with our new foster son. No instruction manual, no medical history, no information on what he likes or dislikes. I didn't even have his middle name.

That makes a total of six children. In the state of Tennessee that is a full house. We are complete and full to the brim. So I thought.

The phone rang early the next morning. The worker wanted to give me a little insight. She told me Baby Jay had a brother and he needed a home. They thought he could stay where he was, but it was not working out. "Can you take him? We can get special approval for you to have seven children."

By now you might be laughing at me thinking, yes, she is definitely insane. But you know exactly where that little boy ended up. Right in my arms. And although yes, there were days that seemed like complete failures and craziness, God made it clear that His grace was enough.

Our strength definitely was not enough. Our pride definitely was not enough. I couldn't muster enough super mom power to care for seven kids if I tried. Our human efforts of humility couldn't even cover it. There was literally nothing in us that could sustain us. Nothing. Except one thing. And I know it sounds extra churchy and uber spiritual but it's the only thing that can explain how we get through each day. God's grace is enough. It's fresh every single day. It's strong. It gives when I feel like I can't give. And guess what? You have access to that grace, too. No matter how much life keeps taking from you or handing you, you can receive God's grace. It's enough for all you are going through, have gone through, or will go through. But first, we have to be willing to say, "God, I can't do this on my own."

For me it takes a little more pressure than some. I mean, seven children, that is a lot. But I'm finally saying, "HELP ME, GOD!" What does it take for you? Trust me, it's better to just give in early. Give in now. Ask for God's grace. He offers it freely. It's up to us to humble ourselves.

Digging Deeper

Here is what it comes down to. There is a simple way to be sure you are living a faith-filled life covered in grace. It's not going to come from thinking your way through life. A life full of faith will never add up or make sense. God's economy and ways of doing things is different than what our minds can comprehend. Life will throw curve balls like phone calls that change the course of life, losses, wins, and grief. But grace. God's grace is enough. And to get to the point of receiving that grace James gives us some very practical advice in chapter 4.

Read James 4:8-9.

Draw near to God.

What could it look like for you to draw nearer to the Lord than you are right now?

He will draw near to you.

What do you think God drawing near to you looks like?

Sometimes we want God to just fix it. I mean, wouldn't it be great for God to step in and clean it all up. Put families back together. Get rid of addiction. Heal broken relationships. Provide pregnancies in quick time. Write it in the sky. Give money for wants and needs. I mean, that sounds awesome to me. But sometimes God doesn't work on our timeline. Often, His timing is so different from ours that we cannot understand. But He tells us in His Word, His ways aren't like ours.

Read Isaiah 55:8–9. How can you lean into this truth in your current circumstances?

Drawing near to God even when we don't understand proves our faith. It says I believe God, and His higher ways see and know all that is going to happen. He is in control, and I trust Him. Pulling away from Him because we feel unseen or unheard proves what we truly believe. It's little faith that says, "I can't draw near to God because He's not hearing me anyway." Deep faith says God knows and will come through in His way and His time. And I am here to tell you He always comes through. It might not be how or when we want, but it will be perfect. I never thought a newborn and toddler were what I needed when all my big kids were self-sufficient and able to make dinner. But God knew. He took me to a place where I needed Him so desperately that I had to find Him over and over again by drawing near once again.

Apply It

The sweet fellowship between a sinner and the Savior that happens when there's no fix to life is a humble drawing that can only be produced in the deep need of soul and the deep satisfaction of faith. Faith takes you through it all and receives the grace freely offered over and over again.

 Cleanse your hands and purify your minds. **This is the instruction James gives. There is a need for cleansing from sin and purification of thought for the one who is "away" from God. Name a sin or a thought that you know you need to give to God so you can receive His grace.**

Sometimes my thoughts run rampant with all the *what ifs* and *what nows*. Every day I have to decide, God is in control. I am learning not to worry about what if. Not to wrestle with what now. But rather, draw near to God. There in that sweet place of His presence we will find all we need to make it through each day. This is the message James is preaching.

Prayer of Faith

Dear Lord, I want to be near You. I want to say yes when it doesn't make sense and control my thoughts when life is swirling. I cannot make it without You. I need You. In Jesus' name, amen.

Memory Verse

Who *is* wise and understanding among you? Let him show by good conduct *that* his works *are done* in the meekness of wisdom. —James 3:13

Day Five: Faith's Proof

When I think back over James and all he tells the believers, it can almost sound like he is talking to those who don't believe. The reminders and the warnings he shares seem like simple things that a believer would obviously do. But as we read James' message, we can conclude that the believers were struggling just like us. They had days of rich faith and days when their faith was failing.

I want to be a believer who really believes. I want my faith to be strong. Even through the testing and the difficult things, I want to know that I will rise up in faith not fear. I want my words to be words that bless and not curse. I want my life to shine because of Jesus, and not just get by because I'm still alive.

I imagine you are a lot like me. You want your life to make a difference. You don't want to be the lady at church who says things that wound others or the one who someone looks at and wonders if she will ever really rest in her faith and in her God. I want to say yes to God even when it doesn't make sense. You, too, want to be so full of faith that no matter what comes your way, you are strong. You want to live humbly and walk in grace. It's what we all want deep in our souls but living a life like that requires so much. It's a humble life that says, "I can't do it." Rather than strength, it requires weakness. This is why it is so complicated. It's not the way our human minds think. It's opposite of what we are used to believing. While we think we need to be stronger, God's Word tells us it's in weakness where real strength is found.

When we naturally want to do life all by ourselves and accomplish all that we can in our own strength, God is instructing us to sit down, be quiet, and just lean on Him. He teaches us not to worry but rather worship Him and find all we need at His feet. Resting. That is where He wants us all along. But often we only get there after we've run so hard we have no other choice but to collapse beneath Him. I feel this deeply and know too well it's true. Even now as I sit in a hotel room pouring out my heart through words, God is reminding me to rest. Right here. Right now. Take a deep breath. Let the craziness of life go and remember why we live.

It's not enough to say, "I believe in God." Faith is more than our words. It requires living. So many wrestle with the message of James because they don't understand if salvation is by faith alone why James pounds so hard on actions. But it's not so much the actions and it's not so much the faith. It's this—**Real faith acts.** Faith is an action word.

- Whether it's resting at the feet of Jesus or feeding the poor.
- Whether it's lifting its heart in worship or pouring out a little more energy that you don't seem to have to give to those who hurt, faith is living a life knowing there's so much more to this life than what we can see.
- It's saying every day, I believe my life is valuable because God created me with purpose.
- It's choosing to run the race God has for me because I have value and my life will make a difference.
- It's choosing on the hard days to rest in God alone as your strength.
- It's choosing on the good days to rest in God alone because even then He is still all you need.

Faith is not about how much you work, and salvation is not about how strong your faith is. Faith is all about a daily humility that says, it's not about me. It's about Him. I trust Him. He sees me. He knows . . . And I can listen to Him. And He hears me. Therefore I will do what He says.

Digging Deeper

 Read James 4:14. Record your thoughts about the verse.

James reminds us life is short. Therefore, we have a brief opportunity to live full of faith. We can choose to wrestle and worry through or we can live a full, vibrant life. It won't be without pain or sorrow. It won't be perfect. But with God it will be everything.

 Read James 4:15–17.

We have no idea what will happen tomorrow. This requires faith. If we knew we might live differently. If we knew the day of our death, we might rush around doing and saying all the things we want to do and say. If we knew the heartaches, we might give up today. If we knew the victories, we might rush ahead of God and try to get there sooner. Living full of faith says, I trust God *today*. I choose grace *today*. I choose joy *today*. I choose to do right *today*. I choose deep faith *today*.

Apply It

 Read Matthew 6:31–34. Record what God speaks to your heart through these verses.

 How do these verses from Matthew hit home what James teaches?

 When you think of your life, in what ways do you want to live with deeper faith? Perhaps it's in your everyday thought life or maybe you need to change your perspective of what you want God to do and live doing what God wants you to do. I can't tell you what God is telling you. But I can tell you, God speaks. He speaks to His child. I have a feeling He is speaking to you, calling you to live a life of deeper faith. Record what areas of life God is prompting you to live differently in the space provided.

Prayer of Faith

Dear God, I want to live a life that proves my faith. I don't want to waste my time worrying and wondering what will happen. I know You are near and You speak. Help me hear Your voice and obey it. Help me to rely on You every day. When I start living in my own pride, remind me to lower my thoughts to worship You. In Jesus' name, amen.

Memory Verse

Who *is* wise and understanding among you? Let him show by good conduct *that* his works *are done* in the meekness of wisdom. —James 3:13

WEEK
FIVE

Full of Faith When Your World Is Falling Apart

Day One: Faith's Lifespan

Take out your Bible or open your Bible app and read James chapter 5.

I gripped my pen tightly and opened my journal. It was a normal day with heavy circumstances looming. We had held a baby in our arms for months without a real plan for what the future would hold with her. By now you know we are foster parents and have a passion to bring in children who need a soft place to land in an uncertain time in their lives. But along with their uncertain lives brings so much uncertainty for our existing family. We've heard it described as inviting suffering to the kitchen table. Along with the sweet child comes great loss of not being with their family and great uncertainty of where they belong and where they will eventually end up.

One day we are a family of six and the next we are a family of seven or eight or even nine. It just depends. If we say yes to a waiting child, our home fills up and there are no open seats in the van. If we say no to a waiting child, our seats sit empty, and the extra bedroom sits silent. With all these uncertain days, we are forced to exercise an extra measure of faith.

I don't share this to toot our own horn or raise up a banner of pride. Or even advocate to get you to jump on the foster care bandwagon. I share this to bring you into the reality that we all are walking through uncertain times. None of us truly knows what tomorrow will hold. Foster care paints a good picture of this idea of an uncertain future. A child is removed from everything familiar and placed in a stranger's home for an unpredictable amount of time. The uncertainties for everyone involved are numerous. There is no way to predict the future outcome.

You've probably felt this feeling in your own way, too. Maybe through the unexpected loss or the uncertain job change. Perhaps for you it's a relationship you wished for or one that ended in a way you never dreamed possible. You've lived your worst nightmare and now you're sweeping up the pieces of life and hoping for new beginnings and fresh faith that takes you to new places in your heart and mind. You've probably held with great hopes a dream that ends up broken or maybe a piece of your life feels lost. When we try to figure it all out and live with a five-year plan, we will live disappointed. We might even find ourselves depressed seeking help in all the wrong places. If you are reading this book, then you are in the right place. James and I have some more hope to offer you.

Digging Deeper

 Read James 4:13–14. Life is a "vapor." What does this mean to you?

Life is short. Yet sometimes it feels oh so long. It's in the seasons when life feels complicated and drawn out that we need to examine and exercise our faith. If our faith is frail, we will naturally drift away from the Lord. We won't take life's surprises well. We won't lift our heads in praise or prayer. We will sink slowly into a dark pit that will steal our joy and suffocate our pleas for peace. Perhaps this is why James says, life is short. It's just a sweet reminder that this is not the end-all. Life isn't about life at all. It's more about what happens beyond this earth. That thought can feel distant or like a hope that is too far away to truly grasp. If we will take hold of the truth that life is short, we will gain insight into what really matters. We will fill our days with things that are important and valuable.

 Read Psalm 39:5. What does the psalmist compare the length of life to?

Read Psalm 144:4. What does the psalmist compare human life to?

When we think of our lives we rarely imagine the width of a hand or the shadows that come and go. Or even the breath we inhale and exhale. We tend to think of life as so much more. We value life because God values life, but then we come to verses like these. They remind us of just how small our time on earth is. In the vastness of who God is and eternity, our lives are tiny specks. We have a window of opportunity to make our moment count or waste it. In Psalm 90:12, the great patriarch of the faith, Moses says, "So teach *us* to number our days, that we may gain a heart of wisdom." Faith is what makes the difference. Will we live in a way that marks the world with faith and joy that radiates the light of the Lord? Or will we waste our time wondering if God really cares and if He will work it all out? All the while God is on the throne working all things together for good.[1] This gives us sweet hope.

Apply It

As we think about life and the brevity of it, fill in the blanks below. There are no wrong answers.

1. My life is a vapor, therefore I will . . .

2. My life is a vapor, therefore I want to . . .

3. My life is a vapor, therefore with my relationships I choose to . . .

4. My life is a vapor, therefore because of my faith I will . . .

5. My life is a vapor, therefore with my thoughts I will . . .

6. My life is a vapor, therefore with my time I will . . .

Prayer of Faith

Dear Lord, when I think of my life, I want to make it count. I want to use my time to make a difference in this world. I want to share my faith and live by faith so others can see Jesus shining through. When my time for death comes, I want to have no regrets. In Jesus' name, amen

Memory Verse

You also be patient. Establish your hearts, for the coming of the Lord is at hand. —James 5:8

Day Two: Faith's Need

Watching his chest rise and fall, I knew for the hundredth time life was like a vapor. His breath, like a vapor, would soon stop. At any moment his chest would fall for the last time and not rise again. The home I lived in, the new dress I just bought, and the matching earrings no longer mattered in the scope of life and death. My nail appointment did not come to mind. My hair that desperately needed to be colored held no value in that moment. Life and the value of it held my attention in the inhale and exhale of all my dad had been through. These moments of life when you are faced with death cause the heart to evaluate what is absolutely important. It's not the farmhouse remodel, the fashion forward outfit, or the scale that says I gained or lost. What matters most is the faith I fall on when my world falls apart.

I know you've been there. Your world has crumbled at some point. You've probably held pieces of life wondering how to put them back together. At moments there is a song or a sermon that offers just what you need to push through, but the only thing that will sustain you through the strong push of fear and life falling apart is rich faith.

Rich faith isn't about money, or homes, or acreage. It's about a person who learns the value of a life lived for Jesus. **When we gather too much stuff, we don't have room for the Savior.**

While faith won't sit on the shelves of your living room bookcase, or be stored in the cabinets of your kitchen, it will be stacked up in your soul. The more faith that is filling your soul, the more strength you will have when you are sitting in the seat of the sufferer. And you will sit there. Perhaps you are even there right now.

As you take inventory of your faith, look for patterns in your need for property or personal gains. Evaluate if you seek stuff more than Jesus. I'll be the first to admit, I so often get this wrong. I find myself sinking into the dark pit of online shopping looking for a cute outfit, a new way to organize my pantry, or a bigger and better house that will meet my heart's desires. When all along the real hole in my heart isn't the shape of a new dress or a new home. It's the exact shape of a deeper relationship with Jesus. With its wide breadth and its deep roots, I see a faith-sized hole so big that nothing I own or want to own could fill it. With each breath of life breathed I know exactly what I need. But I keep searching this world for fulfillment and reasons to believe rather than the Word of God. He promises to give us what we need, but somehow, I've convinced myself I can manipulate my heart toward more faith.

I want to have deeper faith, but things I can see and touch keep beckoning me as if the enemy knows my weakness. It's so much easier to open my phone and mindlessly scroll through photos of my friends on Facebook or shop till I drop a hundred bucks on stuff I don't truly need. *But*, it will help get my overflowing drawers more organized and give me more room to put more stuff. I smirk because I know you know. We all do. We all sit with our phones drowning us in information, education, and experts who have exactly what we think we need. When all along Jesus is saying, *I am all you need.* So I close my computer and ask God to give me faith.

We know it, but we don't truly let the truth of knowing God is all we need penetrate our hearts to the point of putting the phone down and letting God give us more faith.

When we look at what James says to the wealthy in James 5:1, we get a glimpse into the dissatisfaction of the soul of the "rich" man. He *"weeps and howls."* Like a coyote in the middle of the night seeking food, the one who seeks wealth on earth will be distraught to the point of weeping and howling. It's not a pretty picture.

It can feel harsh to directly apply this principle to ourselves, especially if you've ever been poor or had trouble putting food on the table. We've been there receiving WIC[2] to feed our babies. In our early years of ministry, money was extra tight with no room to get anything. Even our needs felt hard to fill, but this wealth of the world is not just monetary. It is more about the need in the heart for more. More what? More of anything you don't have. This might look like more food for a poor man or more money for a rich man, but both sit in the same seat of want and desire feeling like they are suffering.

While we can argue food is necessary and more money is just greed, both men sit with the same heart desire for satisfaction. While one needs satisfaction of the body, the other needs satisfaction of success. Both are things God can give and does give. So, we come to a place of tension when we must ask ourselves—do we trust God to be the giver or do we just continue to be the taker?

Do we focus on what *God* can do or on what *we* can do to get our needs met? This right here is what it comes down to. When we know and receive the fact that God meets our every need and is the giver of all we need, we live by faith alone that He will continue to provide and give us exactly what we need when we need it. When we live believing we need to meet our own needs continually, we will scratch, and howl, and scream our way to get the things we think we need.

Sometimes we have the tendency to start seeking our wants and call them needs. With our homes overflowing with stuff and our barns and garages filled to the brim, we howl in the night. Or maybe better said, we search google, Amazon, and Zillow before we lay our heads on pillows and hope to find the perfect thing. All along, God is offering more than what Amazon can deliver to your doorstep.

Here is a perfect picture of faith. It is believing God will do what He says and believing what He will do is exactly what we need. Elizabeth Elliot says it like this, "God has promised to supply our needs. What we don't have now we don't need now."[3] It sounds a lot like what we heard from the psalmist in Psalm 23 when he said, "The LORD is my shepherd, I shall not want." If we are in need, our real need is for more of the Shepherd. The problem comes when we begin to develop a need for more or different things than God Himself.

It could be a different job, a different salary, a different house, or a different relationship. No matter what it is, it is always rooted in not being satisfied with what God has already given you. How do I know? Because I have been there looking for bigger and better things. I've been the one seeking something God never had for me to seek. Instead of seeking bigger and better things, it is time to seek our great God who owns all those things anyway. Life is too short to get this wrong over and over again. One day life might look and feel broken, bruised, and leave you exhausted to the point of wondering how you will get back up. The stuff we've collected will not help. The satisfaction we've gathered through success won't do what we need at that moment. What will matter is the faith that catches you when life knocks you to the ground.

 What would your life look like if you filled your soul with more faith and your life with fewer things? Perhaps you can grab hold of some of the truths we have already learned from James like applying your heart to wisdom or watching your words.

 Does your life look full of faith? When an outsider sees your circumstances, do they see a satisfied soul who seeks God in all things or a struggling Christian who is getting by but always seems to need more or lives in a constant pity party?

These questions are hard to answer because in the depths of our hearts we all want to be full of faith. We want to live devoted to God and His Word. We want faith over fear and love over lust. We want to get it right and live a life that will matter in the end. But it is hard. You are not alone in your struggle to live satisfied and without want. But God gives us the answers to get it right.

133

Digging Deeper

There are a couple of verses that I go to often when I find myself unsatisfied with my earthly possessions or positions. While I love to look at farmhouse makeovers and learn about how to lose weight fast, I know these things we focus on so much are temporary. One day, the house we fill with stuff will be left behind for someone to empty out for the next generation. One day the body we work so hard to keep young will get old. Wrinkles come. Bodies sag. Eyesight fades. Hearing becomes muffled.

There is one thing that will last forever. The spirit will move from death here on earth to life in heaven for those who know Jesus Christ. The things that will be noticed or mentioned in heaven won't be the big fixer upper reveal or the record time in which you lost the weight. It will be the lives you impacted and the hearts you touched. It will be the way you honored the Lord with your time, your talents, your home, your health, and most of all, your heart.

 Read Matthew 6:19–21. Write down why this idea of living for things that matter is so important.

Apply It

 Think about each of these areas of your life and write down one goal for each that has to do with deepening your faith. I will give you an example for each to help you get started.

Your time—My goal: (example) I will limit screen time to one hour per day and increase Bible reading time by ten minutes per day this week.

MY GOAL: I will . . .

 Your talents—My goal: (example) I will use my gift of encouragement to send one encouraging text to someone in need per day.

MY GOAL: I will . . .

 Your home—My goal: (example) I will fill my home with good music that honors God to set the tone and Bible verses on the walls before I look for more cute stuff on Pinterest.

MY GOAL: I will . . .

 Your health—My goal: (example) I will honor God by taking care of the body He has given me and choose an earlier bedtime of 10 pm even when I still have things undone. I know the work will be there tomorrow.

MY GOAL: I will . . .

Your heart—My goal: (example) I will fill my heart with one Bible verse every single day so I can focus on God's truth over what the world is telling me.

MY GOAL: I will . . .

Faith rich in the Word cannot be stolen. It's yours to keep. Sometimes we get so greedy with our stuff, we forget what truly matters. Faith fills a believer full to the brim and everyone wants it, but no one can take it from you once you have it. It sits heavily in the heart of the one who stores it up. It can be shaken and stirred by life events and struggles of the mind, but you have the opportunity to live with deep faith if you want it.

 Is your heart filled to the brim with faith or are other things filling you up?

 What is something you allow to take up space in your heart? Is there anything you can remove that might make it easier to hear from God?

Prayer of Faith

Dear Lord, I want deep faith. I want to live desiring more of You and less of me. When I see things I think I need, help me to remember You are all I need. While it is nice to have nice things, remind me faith is the most important thing. I choose to trust You with my life, my love, my belongings, my home, my health, my income, and my outcome. In Jesus' name, amen.

Memory Verse

You also be patient. Establish your hearts, for the coming of the Lord is at hand. —James 5:8

Day Three: Faith's Growth

"I wish I had it all together like you." My friend's words struck me hard because I didn't have it all together. Oh, how I wish I did, but I had thought the same thing about her. If I could only be as organized as *she is* or as good a mom as *she seems*. If I could go on lots of dates with my husband like she goes on with *hers*. If I could get my house in order like she's done. Over and over, we look around, see the ways others are succeeding, and wonder why we can't keep up. Maybe you know the feeling. Social media is a dangerous place that leads us to feel less than, as if we are missing the mark.

We can pour our hearts into lots of different areas, but there is one thing we can tend to that will never fade away. It takes time to grow and it takes attention and care. It takes intentionality and determination. It's your faith.

The most important thing you can tend to that will help every other area of your life is the faith that resides deep in your heart. If your heart is not growing, your faith will feel like it's fading. Your heart holds a lot of things. As we get older the capacity for what we hold in our hearts gets bigger and bigger. We have bigger wins and bigger losses. We have deeper griefs and amazing victories. We have more struggles and more revelations. Our wisdom hopefully increases and the capacity for what our hearts harbor tends to grow faster than our minds can fathom. Tending and growing the heart is a silent growth that happens and we don't even realize it. Suddenly we wake up one day realizing we've made it through some tough stuff. I have a feeling you can relate. You've got a story and a testimony. You have things that you want to share with others in order to be helpful. You also have things you are not quite ready to share yet. This is because God is tending your heart and it is growing. This tending of the heart is a slow flourishing of faith or if resisted a fading of faith.

Digging Deeper

 Read James 5:8. Write down the main ideas you see in this verse.

The message James is sharing points to a long-term perspective of growth. It's a reminder to not just rush through life and throw your time into this and that—anything and everything you can get your hands on. It's a patient living of devotion. It's a heart that gives itself for a long-term purpose of loving God and others until Christ returns.

This growth is a slow growth that requires daily attention and time. It's not a widespread, stretched-too-thin kind of living. It's a deep roots way of life that knows what it believes and rests in who they are because of who God is.

Apply It

When James says "establish your hearts" (James 5:8), I think of a strong tree versus a weak one. I think of an established faith. One that stands the test of time and tragedy. One that doesn't break when the wind blows or the storm presses in hard. One with deep roots that can't be easily severed. Look up and read Psalm 1. Like the blessed man we read about, an established heart is a strong tree full of fruit. The fruit doesn't come as a happenstance blessing. It's a direct result of faithful tending and fruitful behavior that generates a strong faith.

 Read Hebrews 11:6. Why is it important to tend to your heart and the faith within it?

 What is the result of faith that is not tended to, grown, or established?

 What is a step you can take to tend to your faith today?

As James begins to conclude his message, he reintroduces a thought he mentioned in chapter 1—patience (James 5:8). While I don't love to wait, patience is a foundational key to established, grounded faith.

It's not that patience is a prerequisite to faith, but it is more like a partner. They walk together. While faith works, patience walks beside faith and puts to work a confident, content spirit that is willing to endure to the end.

It's like faith and patience link arms and each tie one leg to each other as if they were going for a three-legged race. You cannot have one without the other. If one is lacking, the other suffers and is held back.

 Read Psalm 27:13–14 and Isaiah 40:31. Write down how these verses could encourage and strengthen your faith in times of waiting.

Prayer of Faith

Dear Lord, help my faith to grow. I want to live a life strong in my faith and wait for Your perfect timing in my life. Help me tend my heart for growth and wisdom. Help me know You are working all things together for good even when I can't see it. Strengthen my faith. In Jesus' name, amen.

Memory Verse

You also be patient. Establish your hearts, for the coming of the Lord is at hand. —James 5:8

Day Four: Faith's Perseverance

We packed everything we might possibly need for a two-week road trip and filled every seat in our minivan. Before we even crossed state lines, my oldest son started feeling sick. I thought perhaps he ate too much or was getting a little gas so I encouraged him that he would be just fine. "Take a deep breath and put a smile on your face. We are going to have fun. No one can get sick. We are going on vacation! We will have fun! Fun! Fun! FUN!"

No matter how determined I was to have fun, my son's belly ache got worse and worse. His pain increased and by the end of our first day, I knew something was seriously wrong. As we pulled up to the emergency room doors, a male nurse stood at the doors and welcomed us. He immediately set my kiddo at ease and got things moving. Within moments, the doctor came into the room and broke the news.

Jaxon had a bowel blockage and a ruptured appendix. It was life threatening and would require emergency surgery. Suddenly our two-week road trip turned into an eight-day hospital stay in South Bend, Indiana.

There are so many things I could tell you about those eight days, but for today I want you to know that even though my plans for a wonderful vacation did not turn out as I planned, God had a plan.

The third night in the hospital I sat beside Jaxon's bed, and I told God how angry I was for making us miss out on our vacation fun. I let God know how upset and hurt I was that He would allow my boy to suffer. I complained and pouted that life wasn't fair. We were supposed to be having fun and finding relief. I picked up my Bible for the first time in three days and reluctantly flipped it open daring God to bless me. I landed in Psalm 34.

> I will bless the LORD at all times; His praise *shall* continually *be* in my mouth. —Psalm 34:1

The words hit me hard as I heard the still small voice of God reach down and say, "Will you bless my name even now, Micah?" I didn't feel like blessing the Lord. I felt more like cursing. I didn't feel like honoring God. I felt more like complaining. I didn't feel like giving praise. I felt more like pouring out all my problems, but God in His greatness reminded me that even in my temporary pain and suffering, He is still good.

He helped me recall all the blessings I had received as a result of this pain. God showed up in ways I never anticipated. The male nurse who met us at the door was a Christian young man. A local pastor prayed with us before surgery. We received free accommodations through the Ronald McDonald House that provides a home-like environment for families with children who require long-term medical attention. They provided breakfast and dinner every single night. While there, we met a godly couple who were there because their son had been in a car accident. As soon as we met, we both knew we needed each other. We bowed our heads and cried and prayed together. It is no coincidence both of our children had unexpected medical emergencies at the same time. God put us together so we could encourage each other.

There are multiple other ways God showed up that week. I could write an entire book about it. But the point I want to make is this: Sometimes just when we think we know what we need, God has something else in mind for us and it might even look like suffering.

Being tired, tested, and torn isn't always all bad when God is in it. I know that is not the easiest truth to absorb. Suffering can feel like enough is enough. It can feel like we can't take one more thing. But God knows exactly what we can and can't handle, and sometimes He gives us what we can't handle so He can show us who He is and remind us how powerful His comfort and truth really are.

Digging Deeper

Read James 5:11.

 Read Job 42:12–17. How does the end of Job's life show God's mercy and goodness? If you are not familiar with Job's story, he lost everything. He didn't just have a bad day or a tough weekend. He lost his children—all ten of them, his possessions, and his health. In light of this, how do the blessings we read about at the end of Job's story encourage you about how God works?

Apply It

It's easy to read a story on a page, even in the Bible and not truly let it penetrate the heart. But as we take a closer look at James' message, we find a formula for living by faith through the good and bad seasons of life. James seems to repeat the message of waiting and persevering. I know this leads us to the question—but how? How do we live in a content patience that trusts God no matter what? Even Job ripped his clothes and grieved. So how are we to live in faith without doubting God or without wrestling with what is really true? It's not that faith never wrestles or wains. It's more about knowing where to turn when the wrestling match begins. It's choosing to follow James' formula so that no matter what comes your way, you are prepared to stand strong in the face of a tired, tested, and torn up life. Here is the formula that will carry us through:

Consider your trials as joy. Thank God for them knowing He will use them to transform your heart and life in a precious way.
Ask God for wisdom when you do not know what to do. He promises to give it.

Use words to bless the Lord and others. Tend to your heart so your words offer hope.

Keep praying and believing God will do what He promises in His Word. He always does.

As we begin to conclude the book of James, take time to fill in each of the questions below:

※ **What is one trial you need to thank God for today?**

※ **What is one area of life you need wisdom right now? Write it down, then take a moment to ask God for it.**

※ **Who in your life needs to hear encouraging words from you? Send a text, make a phone call, write a card, or take them out on a special outing and say those words.**

※ **What do you need to pray about that maybe you have doubted or stopped praying about? Ask God again. Pray again.**

James begins his final words by calling all to pray. Prayer is our lifeline of faith. It's a way to act out your faith by the means of simply humbling yourself to a point of surrender saying, "God, please help me." So as we finish today, may we all ask God for help.

Prayer of Faith

Dear Lord, I need Your help today. You know the deepest hurts I have endured. You know the current suffering and the struggles I wrestle with each day. Please help me see the good things You promise me and remind me to bless Your name even when I feel like cursing. Help me remember Your truth when the enemy tries to tell me lies. God, I need Your help. In Jesus' name, amen.

Memory Verse

> You also be patient. Establish your hearts, for the coming of the Lord is at hand. —James 5:8

Day Five: Faith's Patience

Have you ever wondered—Ok, God, now what?

This is how it felt when I found a lump again. What now? How do we move forward? What do we do? How bad is it? What will tomorrow hold? What if it's bad? What if? What if? What if?

I wish I could tell you I conquered this trial with smooth sailing. I wish I could say I knocked the devil in the teeth and rose to the challenge with grace and faith deeper than my Texan roots. But I didn't. I let my Bible sit closed on the end table. I got angry with God. I read every article on the internet about the possibilities and self-diagnosed myself before I even got into the doctor to find out what it was.

When suffering hits again, it can be hard to know what to do. Do we collapse beneath the weight of the pain, or do we sit paralyzed in shock? Heartache is not a one-way street. Suddenly the path ahead becomes foggy, the rain can beat down so hard there seems to be no road forward, and the slippery mud beneath the feet feels like there's no footing to escape. I've been there. I've walked the wrong road of doubt and defeat.

The outcome was not what I expected. Thank the Lord it was not cancer. It was not dangerous. What was dangerous was my lack of faith that took one hit and slid right into a deep dark pit of anxiety and fear.

I knew better. I knew all the verses. I knew the songs of faith. I knew the prayers to pray. But instead, I wrestled, I pulled the covers up over my head and gave in to the battle that I should have fought.

Digging Deeper

This is a place I imagine you've been, too. Google seems to give us more instantaneous answers than God sometimes, so we go there first. Even though we know better, we still do it.

James gives us a better way. He tells us how to make it through the hardest of hard.

 Read James 5:13–18. What do these verses tell us can be done in the face of adversity?

Sometimes our Bibles sit closed. We know the right thing to do is open it and let God tell us how to move forward, but we don't open it. We might even know the words to pray, and that God is the great physician, the healer, the helper, and the hope of all mankind. But we wrestle with our own thoughts and fears. We think, "What if God doesn't or won't heal me this time?" I think of my dad who wasn't healed on this earth but had to go on to eternity at an age that seemed too young. These realities make us struggle. But God gives us hope and patience to make it through and strength to begin again.

This is what James is all about. It's about learning the truth about our trials. The ones that rip our hearts from corner to corner. Those are the ones that teach us to wait on God, to live satisfied with who He is, to fill up our hearts with faith strong enough to carry us through. These things we go through aren't in vain. They don't just flutter our way. They make us who we are and ignite great faith or snuff it out and threaten to steal everything we've ever believed or hoped for.

Today is not the devil's day to win. Your heart is not his. Neither is mine. So, the next time pain knocks on your door, or heartache creeps into your life, remember what James says. "Indeed we count them blessed blessed who endure."[4]

How does one count joy when life is all out of sorts?

They exercise deep faith.

The kind that runs headlong into the ground and doesn't let go no matter how strong the rain, wind, snow, or sleet. If the tornado threatens to pull up the roots, it stands secure. That is a life that is tired, tested, torn, and full of faith.

It holds on—no matter what. My message to you, dear sister, is this: Hold on! God is doing something great in you if you will just wait. Let patience increase your faith. In the waiting is where we can be found wanting, wondering, or wading in the fullness of who God is. I can sincerely say, He is all I need. But that is not a victory I win every day. I struggle day by day to choose faith again. To tend to my wavering heart again. Every single day we have the opportunity to live, growing our faith or letting go of our faith. It's time to hold onto what you believe and act on what God has spoken to your heart.

Apply It

Write down what you plan to do to increase your faith as a result of what God is teaching you right now. Use the prompts below to get started:

 In my life right now, I am waiting on God to:

 One way I can find joy in the waiting is:

 One promise from God I can claim while I wait is:

Your faith might not be increased magically overnight. But I promise if you apply the lessons we've learned together through these pages, you will be well on your way to tending a heart full of faith. There is no quick fix or magic pill to take you from tired, tested, and torn, to full of faith, but James sure does offer a mighty prescription to head in the right direction. Your life is not over, therefore your purpose is not complete. Your faith is not wasted, it's waiting for you. How you choose to wait, whether under the wings of the Most High, in the shadow of the Almighty, or at the precious feet of Jesus, will determine your faith. And that place might be the most beautiful place you ever experience.

> But without faith *it is* impossible to please *Him*, for he who comes to God must believe that He is, and *that* He is a rewarder of those who diligently seek Him. —Hebrews 11:6

Prayer of Faith

Dear Lord, I want to live a life of vibrant faith. I want to wait well and prove I trust You in every aspect of my life and being. I don't want to waste a day or moment on things that don't really matter. I want to live with roots planted deeply in the right things so when life makes me feel tired, tested, and torn, I can truly and honestly live full of faith. In Jesus' name, amen.

Memory Verse

> You also be patient. Establish your hearts, for the coming of the Lord is at hand. —James 5:8

Endnotes

Week One: Full of Faith When Life Won't Let Up

1. https://www.goodreads.com/work/quotes/121518-keep-a-quiet-heart.
2. Ephesians 2:8–9.
3. https://www.spurgeon.org/resource-library/sermons/a-warning-to -waverers/#flipbook/.
4. James 1:5.
5. 1 Kings 3:9.
6. Jeremiah 29:13.
7. https://www.blueletterbible.org/Comm/guzik_david/StudyGuide2017 -Jam/Jam-1.cfm?a=1147001.
8. 1 Kings 3:7.

Week Two: Full of Faith to Hear from God and Follow Through

1. https://www.blueletterbible.org/Comm/guzik_david/StudyGuide2017 -Jam/Jam-1.cfm?a=1147001.
2. https://www.dictionary.com/browse/gif.
3. https://www.blueletterbible.org/lexicon/g5036/kjv/tr/0-1/.
4. https://www.blueletterbible.org/lexicon/g2980/kjv/tr/0-1/.
5. https://www.blueletterbible.org/lexicon/g3709/kjv/tr/0-1/.

Week Three: Full of Faith When Life Seems Unfair

1. John 3:17.
2. https://www.blueletterbible.org/lang/lexicon/lexicon.cfm?Strongs=G 4864&t=KJV.
3. https://www.blueletterbible.org/Comm/guzik_david/StudyGuide2017 -Jam/Jam-2.cfm?a=1148002.

4. 1 Corinthians 14:33.

5. James 2:12.

6. James 2:13.

7. 2 Kings 16:3.

8. Genesis 22:8.

9. Genesis 22:11–13.

Week Four: Full of Faith When Your Heart Is Tested

1. Philippians 4:6.

Week Five: Full of Faith When Your World Is Falling

1. Romans 8:28.

2. The supplemental nutrition program for *Women, Infants, and Children.*

3. https://www.goodreads.com/quotes/951524-god-has-promised-to-supply -our-needs-what-we-don-t.

4. James 5:11.